Palms, Wine, and Witnesses

Leonard Broom, *General Editor*
L. L. Langness, *Editor*

STUDIES IN SOCIAL AND ECONOMIC CHANGE
Philip H. Gulliver and David J. Parkin, *Editors*

Palms, Wine, and Witnesses

Public Spirit and Private Gain in an African Farming Community

DAVID J. PARKIN

CHANDLER PUBLISHING COMPANY
An Intext Publisher
SAN FRANCISCO • SCRANTON • LONDON • TORONTO

Library of Congress Cataloging in Publication Data

Parkin, David J
    Palms, wine, and witnesses

    (Studies in social and economic change)
    Bibliography: p.
    1.   Giryama (Bantu tribe)   I.   Title.
DT434.E242P37   916.76'23   73–179032
ISBN 0–8102–0452–5

For Micharo

CONTENTS

viii

TABLES

FOREWORD

It is the intention of this series to present monographs each of which deals with a particular group of people, without seeking to define that phrase too narrowly. Monographs focus on, for example, an African ethnic group, a South Asian caste village or group of villages, and the people of a Pacific island. Each monograph is self-sufficient in its own right and not directly dependent on others in the series, and each is written by an anthropologist who has recently carried out field research in the area concerned.

The focus of each study is on economic, political, and cultural changes, their causes, processes, and consequences during the twentieth century among the selected group of people, and with particular reference to the preceding two decades or so. The primary aim is to describe the changes that have occurred and to give an explanation of the processes involved and their implications. Although broader generalizations (including comparative references to cases and processes elsewhere) are not neglected, it is not a major concern of the series to seek to establish or promote a particular theoretical approach or conclusion. Each author is asked to go beyond description and to make an analysis involving theoretical considerations according to his own preferences.

In the preparation of this series we recognized the necessary diversities of research interests and opportunities, and of theoretical orientation, but nevertheless asked each author, as far as possible, to include the following:

a. in relatively brief outline, the description of a fairly clear and relevant socioeconomic baseline from which to present the account of change (for example, immediately prior to the establishment of colonial rule, or of the achievement of independence, or of the introduction of some major, radical innovation of a technological or social nature);

b. an account of the factors responsible for producing and developing changes and of the agencies through which those factors operated; the initial reactions of the people to these factors and agencies, including the perceptions of the people about them;

c. a description and analysis of the various changes, taking account both of time sequences and of different aspects or parts of the society and culture; the identification of key roles such as those of innovator, entrepreneur, and reactionary (we asked for description to be reinforced, if possible, with quantitative data on such matters as crop production, school attendance, religious converts, and voting in elections);

   d. a consideration of sequences of changes within a single field of activity (such as agriculture) and the extent to which there were concomitant changes in other fields of activity (for example, the association of agricultural change with modes of economic cooperation, family organization, religious beliefs and practices, and political action);

   e. a summing up of the processes of change in the context of anthropological theory.

   We encourage each author to make a serious attempt to cover a wide range of social and cultural changes among the selected people, but acknowledge his legitimate preference to emphasize certain processes of change on which he has most data and theoretical interest.

P. H. GULLIVER
D. J. PARKIN

PREFACE

The fieldwork for this study of economic change among the Giriama of Kenya extended between August 1966 and August 1967 and was made possible by the generosity of the School of Oriental and African Studies, London. The fieldwork methods were social anthropological. My wife and I lived for a few months in a small but important trading centre and for the remainder of the fieldwork in a Giriama homestead three miles from the centre. There we became known as the children of Mutumia Johnstone Muramba of Kaloleni, an honour which gives us more pleasure than even he may realise. We thank him for imparting to us some of the wisdom of the Giriama way.

Previous experience had equipped me with a fluent knowledge of Swahili when I went to the field. But, to Giriama men Swahili is a second language, though very close to their own, while to many women it is hardly known at all. Within a few months I had learned sufficient Giriama to carry on individual conversations and at a later date was able partially but not completely to follow group discussion. Where my Giriama was unsuitable, I used Swahili if possible. I did not, therefore, need a formal, paid interpreter. Nor, for various reasons, was it expedient to use an assistant for survey and data collection. For my quantitative data I found it better to use a small sample of neighbours whom I knew well, rather than attempting a more extensive survey. I acquired figures not through any 'interview' technique but over time, as I gradually compiled, with their permission, the life histories of my immediate neighbours. The figures are thus drawn from a 100 percent sample of a somewhat arbitrarily defined neighbourhood.

As always, observation of events and participation in the round of Giriama daily life provided my central anthropological data. From the more feminine viewpoint, I was greatly helped in all this by my wife, locally called Micharo, to whom I dedicate this book, which truly is in large part hers.

Our greatest thanks go to the Giriama themselves, especially to Kahindi Poko, Kenga Mwiri, Samson Ngumbao, and to their most prominent representative, the Honourable Ronald Ngala, who personally and through his ministry eased our entry into Kaloleni. On a more formal note, I would like to acknowledge the assistance of the Kenya Ministry for Economic Planning and Development, with which this study was registered. Finally, I wish to ex-

press my sincerest gratitude to my colleagues at the School of Oriental and
African Studies who read and commented wisely on drafts of this book, Lionel
Caplan, Abner Cohen, and Philip Gulliver, and to Frederick G. Bailey of the
University of Sussex.

Palms, Wine, and Witnesses

1. Introduction

This is a study of economic development among a people who are very aware of change, even though in the eyes of outsiders they have as yet little experience of it. The official government view through the colonial era and in the new one of independent Kenya is that the people—the Giriama—are among the nation's most economically disadvantaged. And, true enough, their *per-capita* income is among the lowest. A second view is that of the Giriama, themselves, who through their own microscope perceive far-reaching changes, which have largely escaped the eyes of successive administrators. This concept of economic development is in the end a subjective experience, however many indices may be imposed from outside. It is an ideology, a way of saying things about changing social relations. As such, it interests the anthropologist who wishes to explore such changing relations and their expression in people's beliefs and ideas.

There have recently been a number of good, grass-roots studies of economic development and entrepreneurship (Belshaw 1965, Brokensha 1966, Epstein 1968, Geertz 1963, Hill 1970, Long 1968, Pitt 1970, to cite a few). This one goes beyond the roots to the very seeds. It takes a small section of the Giriama at a point in time when it may be said to have had an egalitarian economy—that is to say, an economy in which wealth could only be used to amass or maintain supporters but not to confer substantially higher standards of living. It then follows the society through twenty-five years or so of economic growth based on the profitable cash crop of copra, prepared from coconuts. During this period an emerging category of enterprising farmers made long-term capital investments in land rather than in people. But, even at the end of the twenty-five years, the differences between their life style and that of ordinary farmers were not great. Indeed, the enterprising farmers deliberately have kept them uniform. Put another way, they need to continue to subscribe to the "common language of custom," for by strongly emphasising such customary spheres of exchange as bridewealth transactions and reciprocal funerary obligations, they turn them to their own advantage by using them as investment systems. These men are the pace-setters through whose example cash bridewealth and funerary expenditure have become enormously inflated. They themselves face the risk of overspending their resources in these spheres. But those who survive are able to acquire land and economically valuable coconut palms from less prosperous farmers, who must sell or pledge such property in order to raise the cash needed for such

1

contingencies as a household funeral or a male dependent's bridewealth.

Expenditure on such contingencies as these, or more general types of expenditure like conspicuous consumption and potlatching, have been shown in other parts of the world to mark off groups within a society and to constitute a mechanism by which groups acquire, lose, or simply retain their positions of power or privilege.

I am dealing here, however, with a society in which an ideal of contingent and conspicuous expenditure is followed by all men. It is a society which is only beginning to undergo economic differentiation and which cannot yet be said to have internally distinguished corporate groups. It is only a minority of enterprising farmers who constitute a category, socially recognised as such, who regard each other as rivals in a competition to acquire land and palms. But they have not yet come together as an interest group.

However, by focusing on individual enterprising farmers, we are able to see a similarity in their methods of calculating profit and loss in the two investment spheres mentioned (bridewealth and funerary expenditure), as well as in the more obviously contractual sphere of land and palm transactions. We see also that they are faced with a common dilemma. On the one hand, they must subscribe to the common language of custom as a means of placing and controlling their investments. On the other hand, their long-term aims are to expand and diversify their economic enterprises and reduce their dependence on farming and so to lessen the amounts they spend in the two customary spheres.

By using the image of an entrepreneurial ladder, I am able to observe men gradually shifting their resources away from the two customary spheres and investing them in more profitable enterprises. They do this *not* by severing their ties with the local community of which they are members, but by taking a stand on certain issues of custom or law. In other words, they modify some of the customary norms surrounding the spheres of exchange. This enables them to continue to operate with impunity in the society, but marks them off as men who now have the economic power to do a little more as they please. They have purchased an iota of privilege.

At the top of the entrepreneurial ladder, we have a few examples of men who, under the special circumstances of political independence in Kenya, have been able to turn to the state to acquire the legitimacy needed to run their businesses. I am less concerned with these, who are the full fledged traders who characteristically figure in studies of entrepreneurship; I am more concerned with enterprising farmers, who are grappling with the problem of how to introduce new idioms into ths common language of custom without going so far as to cut themselves off from the contacts needed in the competition for palms and land. Contacts, in the form of men who will provide information on property available for sale and who will witness its purchase, are absolutely necessary for two related reasons. The first is that there is no government land or tree registration among Giriama. Though the selling and mortgaging of property has been practised by Giriama for many years, none of it is recorded in official quarters, even though in recent years very valuable transactions have taken place. Men thus need witnesses to testify in the government court or neighbourhood moot that they have legitimately acquired a piece of land or some palms. A second reason for needing contacts is that there must be a means by which a potential buyer can be informed of available property and by which he can measure his performance against that of rival enterprising farmers; for it is known that the more successful a rival, the better his network of witnesses and informers and the greater his chances of snapping up a bargain.

This sort of situation may give rise to the formation of cliques or factions around an enterprising individual, but even here the Giriama enterprising farmers differ. They already invest heavily in promoting inflation in bridewealth and funerary expenditure and have not yet acquired the resources to act as true patrons in dispensing regular benefits to a band of followers. Instead, each retains no more than a constantly shifting loose-knit network of contacts, who in no sense constitute a face-to-face or organized group able to exert pressure on him. The more successful an enterprising farmer becomes, the more likely are his contacts to come closer together and to regard him as a source of patronage. How, then, docs he ward off such intensity of involvement, which would threaten to drain his resources?

There operates in this event what we might call the principle of ritual distinctiveness. A number of successful farmers and entrepreneurs who are subject to intense pressures of this kind undergo possession by a so-called Islamic spirit. After diagnosis by a diviner whose verdict is commonly accepted, they are obliged to "become Muslim," to the extent only of observing the fast of Ramadhan and the Islamic prohibition on alcohol and the meat of animals which have not been slaughtered by Muslims. Palm wine is drunk daily by Giriama, and collective meat-eating ceremonies are frequent and intense. A consequence of this release from close commensal relations is that it signifies and categorizes the relationships between a successful farmer and his ordinary neighbours and friends, who may include witnesses and informers. A measure of ritually sanctioned distinctiveness is thus achieved at an interpersonal level.

This is a limited example of a more general process of conversion to an "outside" religion as a means of legitimating non-customary activities and expectations. Thus, Long (1968) shows how in a Zambian rural community enterprising farmers tend to become Jehovah's Witnesses and selectively appeal to that religion to justify their departures from economically unprofitable relationships.

The converse occurs when an already established group of traders re-emphasises or redefines its own religion. Thus, the entrepreneurial groups studied by Geertz (1963) in two Indonesian towns do not undergo conversion to a new religion, but instead stress the propriety and distinctiveness of their own interpretations of, in one case, Islam and, in the other, Hinduism. More recently, Abner Cohen (1969a) shows how a group of Hausa traders in the Nigerian town of Ibadan preserve their autonomy not only by stressing their internal Hausa distinctiveness from other groups in the city, but also by moving outside their society to latch onto a particular Islamic order, the Tijaniyya, whose ritual practices admirably suit the needs of ambitious traders. The Indonesian and Hausa cases are examples of the strategies which interest groups may adopt in the face of competition with other groups, the full theoretical implications of which are spelled out by Cohen.

But in the Zambian community described by Long and among the Giriama described in this study, the greatest struggle facing enterprising farmers is with members of their own community, the ever-demanding kin and neighbours. The analysis is thus focused not on the relations between distinct cultural groups, but on relations between individuals as members of social categories of a single cultural group. This closer focus is presumably implicit in the title of Long's study, *Social Change and the Individual*, and in his plea for studies of individual cases of conversion. Of course, we must not, as Cohen warns (1969b), overuse the microscope to observe individuals' motivations to the exclusion of the groups or categories of which they are members. There is a useful half-way stage at which we can analyse the ways in which particular key roles in a society change in content and definition as they respond to alterations in the society's wider structure of economic and political relations.

The present study focuses on the mediatory roles of those designated as elders. As mediators, elders uphold and sanction the principle of household authority according to agnatic seniority. But they also act as witnesses and thereby sanction the increasing tendency among enterprising farmers to buy land and palms without reference to agnatic relationships and—frequently—in the face of them. The elders' mediatory roles thus support conflicting principles for allocating property.

It is also the case that the new, enterprising farmers are frequently designated as young. There is undeniably a cleavage developing between accumulators and losers of property. But this cleavage between rich and poor men is frequently spoken of by Giriama as a conflict between homestead heads who are young and those who are elders. This is interesting because intergenerational differences of behaviour have always received great symbolic expression among Giriama, though the forms of particular symbols have changed over the decades. I suggest here that this symbolisation of intergenerational differences hides the cruder and less customarily acceptable cleavage between a rich "capitalistic" minority and a poorer majority. The mediatory roles of elders and their sometimes parallel roles as ritual specialists and doctors play crucial parts in this process of symbolisation. These culturally recognized roles can themselves be seen as symbols, in that they mediate contradictory principles. Thus, on the one hand, the roles support what are publicly said to be time-honoured and custom-hallowed agnatic and gerontocratic principles. On the other hand, by acting as links with the government courts and development agencies, the roles implicitly legitimize the efforts of men who most flout agnation and gerontocracy. The argument may be summed up in a parody of Leach (1954, p. 278): arguments about age differences and ritual privilege among this section of Giriama are arguments about emerging wealth differences.

More generally, this study attempts to make a contribution to the problem of the relationship between what Merton (1957) originally called manifest and latent functions of institutions. Here I deal with key institutionalised activities and roles which, through an exaggeration of their culturally prescribed and publicly recognized forms, actually mask underlying developments of a new and radical nature.

Argument and Layout of this Book

In Chapter 2 I describe the development from cattle-grazing to coconut-palm agriculture in one Giriama area. The switch to palms involved Giriama inextricably in the international economy. Wealth differences now had more permanent and radical implications. The arrival of Kenya's independence and the state's positive involvement in local entrepreneurial farming has accentuated the apparent permanency of wealth differences: the larger, encapsulating political system is now nibbling at the local-level one (see Bailey 1969, 144ff.). Nevertheless, the local-level system persists in the waning, but still important power of elders, whose stated support for an egalitarian distribution of property is expressed, among other ways, in the agreement among neighbours to buy and sell palm wine on a virtually profitless basis.

In Chapter 3 I discuss a Giriama neighbourhood in which we see precisely what the powers are which, even under contemporary conditions, elders can wield, and in Chapter 4 I describe the new capitalistic forces which threaten them. I dwell on these forces in Chapter 5, stating that, land, palms, and other trees are increasingly being acquired through sale and mortgage for purposes of capital accumulation. A minority is accumulating the primary means of production. Why, then, does the majority sell? And why is the emerging economic cleavage conceptualised in cultural terms as an intergenerational one?

In Chapter 6 and 7 I suggest an answer to these questions. I describe two main sources of contingent or essential expenditure: bridewealth and funerary expenditure. Both have become sharply inflated in recent years as a result of involvement in the international market. The interesting feature of these is that they have ambivalent consequences, rather like the mediatory roles of elders. From one point of view, they can be seen simply as spheres of economic consumption which exist to satisfy the demands of status and honour among individuals and families. But from another point of view, they are spheres of investment. For poor men they are consumption spheres, in that they provide little more than the hollow return of satisfied honour and economic bankruptcy. But for richer men they are the means by which support and information can be bought and, in the struggle to acquire palms and land, may in the end provide tangible returns. I call them investment spheres, not because they may involve conscious, rational calculation (which is difficult to substantiate) but by reference to their consequences. Individual motivations do vary, but for Giriama the overall social justification for such expenditure is said to be the satisfaction of honour, the loss of which does, it is clear from observation, invite scorn or pity.

In ways which I explain, both spheres can be seen by Giriama to uphold the gerontocratic and agnatic principles. It is this which enables us to understand why influential Giriama elders continue to bankrupt themselves and their families and why, therefore, the developing economic cleavage is said to involve a conflict of adjacent generations.

In Chapter 8 I show how the encapsulating state political structure and inextricable involvement in the international market are providing the conditions for the formation of minor family dynasties. Factors of the domestic life cycle are becoming less important in the formation of wealth differences and the inter-generational expression of economic cleavage will thereafter be less suitable. A cleavage expressed along the lines of class seems more likely in the near future, as the minority of land and palm accumulators begins also to occupy the commercial positions vacated by Asians, who are leaving Kenya.

In conclusion, I suggest that the mediatory roles of the elders, the idiom of an intergenerational conflict, and the heavy expenditure on bridewealth and funerals are paradoxes of custom: in the short term they seem to maintain the *status quo* of custom and authority and so are publicly approved, but in the long term they serve to mask the development of a fundamental cleavage.

2. Redistributional and Capitalist Economies

In this opening chapter I explain how Giriama switched from primarily subsistence farming to a dependence on cash-cropping, yet retained a dominant ethos of sharing, in the face of a more individualistic organization of economic relations. I turn first to the ecological origins of this switch.

Movement and Settlement

Ranged over 5,000 square miles of the Kenya coast and its immediate hinterland and pushing south for a little way along the Tanzanian coast are the Mijikenda. The Mijikenda or Midzichenda, as they are called in the local vernaculars, number at least 350,000 and comprise nine sub-groups with mutually intelligible dialects and very similar customs. The largest is the Giriama, who number over 150,000 and occupy a mainly hinterland area of 2,500 square miles.

During the colonial regime—from 1888 to 1963—the Giriama were labelled conservative, economically backward, or, more romantically, independently spirited. Like most subjective evaluations, these hide the real reasons as to why these peoples resisted what was regarded by the colonial administrators as economic progress. Two general reasons may be suggested. One is that the Giriama already had efficient trading relations among themselves, with neighbouring Mijikenda peoples, and with coastal Arabs and Swahili. They thus showed a high degree of economic self-sufficiency and did not need to adopt new techniques of farming for cash crops or to migrate in large numbers to work in towns or on plantations. A second reason is that such economic expansion as occurred in the early colonial period was largely confined to the immediate coastal belt, which was controlled by Arabs and, to a lesser extent, Europeans. Giriama could only offer themselves as labour on plantations of which they could never become owners. Arab and later European ownership of plantations and other economic enterprises had been given legal and constitutional support by the British administration under a coastal protectorate agreement in 1895, by which the Sultan of Zanzibar was declared ruler of a ten-mile coastal strip.

An abortive Giriama rebellion against the British in 1914 marked a point at which Giriama were unable to maintain their autonomy. They were thereafter obliged to pay taxes regularly and supply migrant labour. The number of Giriama who did migrate for wage labour has never been considerable, compared with some neighbouring peoples, but migrant labour was a useful, if disliked, means of acquiring cash to supplement traditional trading. This traditional trade had operated most freely in the nineteenth century before 1895, when the British government imposed the protectorate. The trade had consisted of barter with Mambrui and Mazrui Arabs. The Giriama would offer grain or ivory for cloth or money. They would use the money to buy palm wine from a neighbouring and culturally close people called the Rabai, who specialised in planting coconut palms which they later tapped for palm wine. Under British rule, from 1895 ivory trading was outlawed, and by 1914/1915 the high exports of Giriama grain appear to have dwindled considerably.[1] Clandestine ivory trading appears to have continued but could not meet the increasing need for cash among Giriama, who now had to pay taxes regularly as well as satisfy a growing demand for palm wine.

These needs might have been filled if larger numbers of Giriama had migrated as wage-labour to towns like Mombasa or Malindi or to the Arab- or European-owned plantations of sisal and other cash crops. But Giriama did not do this on any appreciably increased scale. Instead, they exploited suitable areas of their natural environment. In the early twenties, only a few years after the abortive rising, large numbers began to repeat a pattern of earlier generations by migrating to more southerly Giriama lands in what is now southern Kilifi District, an administrative division of 94,133 persons in 1962, more than a third of them, Giriama.[2] Five other Mijikenda peoples live in southern Kilifi, including the Rabai, who were and are masters of palm-wine production. There coconut palms grow well and can be tapped successfully. Those Giriama who migrated to this general area in the early twenties appear to have been attracted by the possibility of planting and growing their own palms and so having their own sources of wine. This was thus one means of meeting the need for palm wine.

Migration to an area fit for palms also went some way toward solving the problem of raising cash. Copra, the dried and prepared coconut flesh, was a cash crop in the East African coastal area by the beginning of the twentieth century. In the 1930s the southerly Giriama who were successfully growing palms also began to produce and sell copra to Asian merchants residing among them, who acted as middlemen. It seems that these Giriama imitated the neighbouring Rabai, who had been producing copra and palm wine since the turn of the century.

This study is set in one such area in which Asian shopkeepers and traders settled and in so doing involved Giriama in an external economic market in copra. More than this, these Giriama have become involved in a change during the past thirty years from a primarily redistributional economy based on palm wine to an accumulative or capitalist one based on copra (and coconuts).[3] By redistributional (cf. Dalton 1954) I mean an economy in which earned cash must at some point be mainly invested in the "purchase" of people for support. By capitalist I refer to the increasing use of cash for the purchase of the primary means of production without a corresponding increase in the need to "buy" supporters.

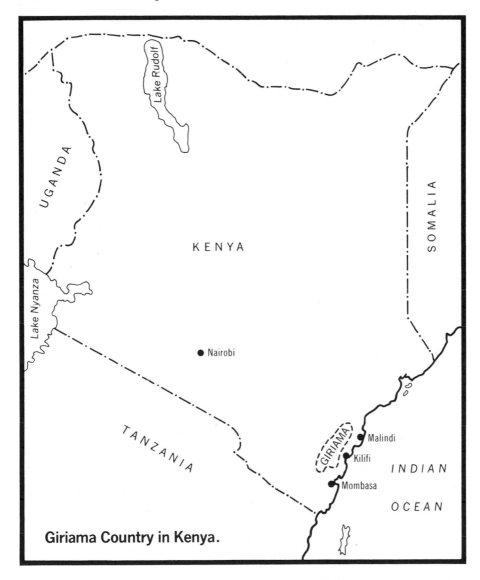

Giriama Country in Kenya.

The area in which all this occurred is called Kaloleni. It is situated thirty miles inland from the major East African port town of Mombasa. Kaloleni is the name for a trading centre of twelve Asians, ten Muslim Swahili, and six Giriama shops, stalls, and tea-houses. The importance to Giriama of the Asians and Swahili will emerge later. Kaloleni trading centre also has a farmers' co-operative, a mission hospital,[4] and a government district office and court. Kaloleni is also the name for an administrative location of 12,785 persons (1962 Kenya census) in an area of 29 square miles (441 persons per square mile). It is part of southern Kilifi

District, for which the importance in 1966 of copra and coconuts as cash crops is shown by the following figures:[5]

	Produce exported	Estimated Income
Palms	{Copra	K£ 36,590
	{Coconuts	£ 25,366
	Cashew Nuts	£ 11,157
	Cotton	780

Palm Wine and "Sharing"

Let me show how the trade in palm wine involves a redistributional economy, while that in copra is part of an expanding capitalist one. The trade in palm wine has never been specifically encouraged by the governmental administration and, on occasion, has been actively discouraged. On the whole, however, the Mijikenda have been left to develop their own highly complex system of producing and distributing the wine. Under these conditions of production and distribution, palm wine cannot be bottled or kept for more than a day or so. Palm wine cannot therefore be hoarded until periods of scarcity for the purpose of securing a higher price. There are regular regional differences in price, but, otherwise, price fluctuations are determined only by seasonal factors. The technical difficulties of rapid distribution necessitate a complex organisation of expert manpower, from tapping the individual palms, to placing the collected wine into unstopped gourds, to carrying it to a bus stop for transportation for sale in an area where palms do not grow, to arranging to have it sold and the money (minus a commission) returned to the producer. All this has to be done within a couple of days. It can only be done through the use of many men—tappers, carriers, loaders, a trusted bus driver, and a selling agent.

The production and distribution of palm wine thus makes the large-scale producer, who is an enterprising farmer or entrepreneur, dependent on a local and neighbourhood labour force. Being so dependent and being at the same time in competition with rival producers who are also local men, places a premium on cordial relations with the men who constitute the labour force. The men of this labour force are also farmers. The most important, the tappers, are always employed by more than one employer. Some tappers themselves employ tappers. The main point is that, as well as being farmers, the tappers are neighbours both to each other and to the Giriama entrepreneurs. They always refer to each other by kinship terms.

Thus, the crudely contractual element in the relationship is suppressed terminologically. It is also suppressed in behaviour and in the nature of payment: if a tapper appears inefficient or lazy, his employer never formally discharges him, but suggests that another tapper help him in his work; a tapper's payment is a fixed proportion of the wine he has tapped, which he himself may sell, so that his rewards are commensurate with his labours.

In addition to all this, the Giriama entrepreneur who is a large-scale producer of palm wine has to be careful to sell his wine beyond his own locality, except on festive occasions or when supplies are low, preferably sending it by bus to the non-palm areas. He must exercise care to do this because he must not compete with the many small-scale farmers who own at least some palms which are tapped.

These small-scale farmers sell to and buy from each other at different times, as wine is made available. These are cash transactions, but, overall, few small farmers make significant profits. It is clear that, like the relationship of the tapper to his employer, this economically profitless circulation of palm wine and cash expresses the existing pattern of such primary ties as kinship, affinity, and neighbourhood.

A normative rule, allegedly enshrined in customs, reinforces this ethos of egalitarianism. Men may never tap their own palms. Even the poorest of men with very few palms must summon the help of men outside his family, while he himself may, if he wishes, tap other men's palms. Giriama explain that this is a way of ensuring that all men have work. In a sample of forty homesteads in the Kaloleni area only one included a man who had tapped his own palms. But he claimed to be on the lookout for an available tapper and subscribed to the system in that he also tapped the palms of two neighbours, who were not able to tap for him.

As well as being drunk daily, palm wine is used on all ceremonial occasions, of which the longest, most lavish, and most heavily attended are funerals. Palm wine is thus a commodity used both on local festive occasions and in transactions between neighbours, all of whom, by classificatory extensions, can be referred to alternatively as kin or affines. In agreeing to divert the sale of his own palm wine outside this face-to-face community and so allowing wine and cash to be exchanged at no significant economic profit, the Giriama entrepreneur is seen to subscribe to the ethos of egalitarianism, or, as Giriama put it, to "sharing".

For ordinary farmers, then, this profitless sphere of exchange makes a nice empirical correspondence with the ideology of sharing. Entrepreneurial farmers who do make profit from this trade nevertheless do not rely on it exclusively. They have turned to copra as their main cash crop.

But what of the few now elderly Giriama men who achieved wealth in the recent past through success in the wine trade before the switch to copra? Why were they involved in a redistributional rather than a capitalist economy? First, their absolute dependence on neighbourhood help required them to "feed" local supporters. They could help men with direct financial loans. More commonly they would agree to marry a poorer man's child-daughter or -sister and so provide him with the considerable bridewealth, which increasingly consisted of cash in more modern times (see Chapter 6). Success in the wine trade, therefore, came to be equated with having many wives. Apart from overloading a family estate with too many sons, this necessary heavy investment in local support inevitably diverted money from the purchase of more palms, so that rates of palm accumulation by individual families were slow, compared with those in recent times.

Second, however, the fact that palm wine has rarely been exported beyond the Mijikenda area prevented the trade from bringing in significant supplies of new cash. Compared with the present trade in copra, the trade in palm wine did little more than stimulate the circulation of cash already in the society, which trickled in slowly from a low rate of migration for wage-labour and from limited trade in other commodities. This was an internal economy, in which cash was used for redistributional rather than capitalist purposes.

The present trade in copra and coconuts contrasts with this in five respects: First, copra and coconuts have always been sold to Asian and Arab firms in Mombasa, except for some coconuts which have been sold as palm seeds to other Mijikenda. Before independence Asians in Kaloleni and a few Giriama acted as middlemen to effect this sale of produce to Mombasa. After independence this was done by the local Kaloleni farmers' co-operative. While the Asians, most of whom are not citizens, have gradually been squeezed out of this market, the Giriama entrepreneurial farmers have been able to compensate for their lost role as middlemen and have instead been able to buy up large fields of palms. A minority of Giriama have thus begun to accumulate the most important means of production in their community.

Second, the trade involves an exported commodity and is very dependent on international market factors.[6] Third, because copra is an export, cash received for it is not acquired as a result of an existing system of redistributional political and economic obligations. It does not, therefore, have to be fed back into the system of reciprocal obligations and can be earmarked as surplus money for the purchase of new palm trees. Fourth, copra does not involve the same problems of production, distribution, and sale as palm wine. While palm wine has to be sold within a day or so of being tapped, copra can be prepared at a more leisurely pace from felled coconuts, and, though neighbourhood help is needed for the felling, that aid does not play as crucial a part in the process of production, distribution, and sale as it does for palm wine. Finally, unlike the trade in palm wine, the copra trade has received government encouragement. It is relevant now to ask what the nature of this encouragement has been.

To this point I have distinguished two modes of economic activity—redistributional and capitalist. The Giriama themselves make a parallel distinction between sharing and accumulation, claiming that the former alone is traditional and therefore desirable. People agree about this—in their statements, at least. Why is there consensus at this level, while at another, more fundamental level people are becoming increasingly separated into rich and poor, as individuals manipulate the economic opportunities? The general agreement about the desirability of Giriama tradition is, in fact, based on a common need to observe certain customary rules of mediation: elders need mediatory roles to sanction their own positions; enterprising farmers need witnesses and mediators to support and settle their claims.

Protection in Law

There are two important kinds of encouragement which the government can provide to enterprising farmers. One is agricultural development loans. The second, in Kaloleni, is to register and consolidate the land and trees in the area. But, although some loans have been made available since Kenya's independence in 1963, land and trees have not yet been registered. This has meant that the sanctity and protection of customary law has continued to be crucially valuable to enterprising farmers, even since the switch to the use of palms for copra and coconuts as main cash crops.

In the scramble for land and palms during this twenty-five years, men have had no alternative to recruiting their own witnesses from among neighbours and relatives who will testify to ownership or rights in land or trees. Title deeds are not issued, and oral testimony has been used more frequently than written documentary evidence during this period of (according to government reports and informants' statements) increased land litigation.

As in many parts of colonial Africa, neighbourhood moots have been allowed and frequently have been encouraged to operate alongside government courts, offering possible preliminary "out-of-court" settlements. Now, as before, neighbourhood witnesses in Kaloleni may testify at both levels, if called. They do so within the juridical framework of Mijikenda custom. As in much of Africa, it is frequently the household heads of some seniority who are looked upon as the most reliable witnesses.

The concept of "elder" *(mutumia)* among Giriama is far from being outmoded. It is crucially relevant to contemporary activities. Mijikenda customary law, as exercised in the government court, in local moots, and through branches of the politically significant Mijikenda Union, supports the gerontocratic principle.[7] Without being formalised as among the East African societies with institutionalized age groups (e.g. Gulliver 1963, Spencer 1965), this subsumes agnatic seniority as a complementary principle of allocating authority. For instance, in disputes over economically important matters such as the ownership of palms and other trees, land, moveable heritable wealth, or bridewealth, elders from different clans or descent lines, but often of the same neighbourhood or locality, will be called in to testify as to entitlement. Since they are themselves agnatically senior within their own families, they will normally have a vested interest in phrasing their entitlement in terms of agnatic seniority, however divided they may be about who is actually the most senior of the claimants.

Enterprising farmers, who tend to be younger than court or moot elders, are thus obliged to operate within the framework of a local gerontocracy and of certain rights being awarded on the basis of agnatic relatedness. Yet, during the period of economic changes in Kaloleni, they have increasingly pursued a straight contractual principle of buying and selling land and palms on an individual basis, without reference to agnatic entitlement. But this emphasis of enterprising farmers on personal achievement has actually been facilitated through the statuses of the elders. On one hand, the legitimacy for their status as elders rests on continued recognition by the government court and the administration of Mijikenda customary law, of which agnation is a key principle. On the other hand, they are called in additionally as witnesses for transactions of land and palms which involve outright sale or mortgage and which ultimately enable more such property to be concentrated in the hands of a minority of younger, enterprising farmers. In other words, through the mediatory roles of the elders, the society is undergoing radical economic change. This ambivalent power of the elders has been possible because Mijikenda customary law is not yet constituted into a written legal code and so has remained broadly defined.

Mijikenda Customary Law: the Government Court

The government courthouse in Kaloleni is sited within the administrative compound. The magistrate and clerks are all Giriama and, like the chief and sub-chiefs, are appointed to their positions on permanent pensionable terms. In recent years, younger, educated magistrates have been appointed, who have had to undergo some formal legal training. As before, Mijikenda custom, as it is called in court, still constitutes the body of legal rules and precedent referred to in actual cases. But interpretation of this custom has evolved in accordance with the economic and social changes which have occurred as a result of the extension of the palm belt.

Enterprising men tend to innovate, not only by setting new life styles or by indicating new sources of economic and political influence, but also as litigants posing new problems which require unprecedented solutions. In spite of this constant modification, Mijikenda custom remains the basic body of rules to which reference is made in both litigation and adjudication. Mijikenda custom remains broadly defined because it is used to settle cases between most of the Mijikenda sub-groups in Kilifi District, which nevertheless show slight differences of emphasis on such matters as inheritance, bridewealth transactions, and the legitimacy of offspring.[8] These differences are always minor, however, and are easily accommodated within what Hoebel (1940) has called the broad "law-ways". Kaloleni court is used mostly by Giriama, but people of nearby Mijikenda sub-groups use it also, and this obliges the magistrate and clerks to retain the broad conception of Mijikenda custom.

Mijikenda Customary Law: the Elders' Moots

The notion and use of Mijikenda custom also operates in important moots made up of notable local elders. For most of us the term *elder* tends to have the connotation of traditional diehard. Frequently, however, Giriama elders are men who understand well the persuasiveness of arguments based on pleas for conservatism. They emphasise the virtues of old ways not simply out of blind reverence for them, but often because their own positions of authority and influence in the small-scale society rest on an unchallenged claim to powers of mediation and arbitration. Both are frequently achieved through the use of ritual. Local moots are thus alternative places for litigation where decisions or advice may lack the backing of the state, but, as I shall show, are supported by the sometimes more binding force of mystical belief.

Far from disappearing as a result of economic change, the local moots in Kaloleni have increased in importance in recent years. They offer a cheaper level of litigation, which people may prefer to the more expensive government court, with its system of costs and fines. While the government court may nowadays be said to offer potentially greater benefits to the entrepreneur who wishes to reformulate custom, the local moots are bastions of non-entrepreneurial influence. The recently emerging division between richer and poorer men has increased rather than diminished the need for such platforms of influence. But because they, in effect, take business away from the government court and because their pronouncements frequently extol the use and value of ritual oaths, the government court has inevitably clashed with them.

The conflict between these two is a manifestation of a normally much less obvious growing cleavage between those persons acquiring palms and other economic enterprises and those who are losing palms and land. This is because the elders who sit on the moots may be regarded as representatives of the majority of local farmers who are not accumulating palms and who may in fact be losing them through sale to enterprising farmers. These elders are without substantial palms or other economic assets. The knowledge and application of customary law, reinforced by ritual expertise, is their greatest resource. Lacking government sanctions to apply their interpretation of customary law, they attempt to tap the power of indigenous mystical belief and practice, particularly through the use of oaths. This said, enterprising and ordinary farmers do not face each other in a state of naked hostility. It must be remembered that the enterprising farmers here discussed are insiders, members of the Giriama community in which they were born and raised. Consciously or unconsciously, they have to express some deference to the elders, if only in order to retain their support as witnesses and thus continue to expand their holdings. This is the enterprising farmer's dilemma: he must not seem to flout custom too harshly lest he fail to achieve or retain the local clientele on which his success depends; yet, to succeed, he must excel among his fellows in progressively acquiring their palms and land, in doing which he may be accused by elders and others of contravening certain customary expectations.

Conflicting expectations of this kind between enterprising and ordinary farmers are ideological arguments about which customs should be retained and which discarded. The two spheres of the palm-based economy are used by elders to illustrate this ideological gulf. The production and sale of copra is often said to have weakened Giriama self-sufficiency by tying them to external market forces of supply and demand. By contrast, the production and sale of palm wine, which is internal to Mijikenda, is set up as an example of traditional egalitarianism. As I explained, it underlies an ideology of sharing.

The ideology of sharing is in turn used as a moral weapon by elders to admonish enterprising farmers who relentlessly acquire palms and land. And yet, those same elders will agree to act as witnesses on behalf of such expansionist farmers. This illustrates further the ambivalence in their role. They sanction rights in property which uphold custom—namely, those based on agnation—but sanction also those acquired through purchase or mortgage, which may be said to contest custom. I shall now outline these rights and, in doing so, introduce the small neighbourhood in Kaloleni on which this study is focused.

NOTES

1. *Kilifi District Political Records.* This document, *The Kilifi District Gazeteer* compiled by W.F.P.Kelly in 1960, and the *Annual District Reports* for Kilifi District and Malindi Sub-district provide some general historical information to which I make occasional reference. These sources are lodged in the Kenya Archives, Nairobi, except where otherwise stated.

I should mention here that Mr. F. Morton has recently completed a focused historical study of Mijikenda, while two other historians, Mrs. C. Smith and Mr. T. Spear, are at present engaged in work on colonial and pre-colonial history, respectively.

2. Earlier migration and palm growing are suggested by W.E. Taylor's comment in 1891 that southern Giriamaland, or Weruni, was "once thickly populated, as is evidenced by numerous deserted palm-groves and sites" (p.a3).

3. At the same time their dependence on cattle for subsistence and for use as bridewealth has lessened (see Chapter 5).

4. Though the Christian Missionary Services station was built in 1904 and its hospital in 1929, few Giriama are even nominal Christians at present. Coastal health hazards and Giriama economic and cultural self-sufficiency have in the past limited conversion. Therefore, since education tended to follow missionary successes, few Giriama over the age of forty are now literate. Of 450 heads of homestead around the trading centre, 27 percent use at least one Christian name for taxation and other official purposes. Except for a further 6 percent who are Muslim and so are obliged to use Muslim names, all others use only Giriama names. Use of a Christian name by these heads denotes in all cases to my knowledge a couple of years of formal school education, though rarely more.

5. Taken from the 1966 Kilifi District, southern division, report. See also Taylor, D.R.F., 1970 for an account of the distribution of cash crops by trading centres in Kilifi and other districts. One Kenya pound (K£) was worth two dollars and eighty cents, American, in 1966.

6. As indeed it apparently was during World War I in Rabai District, where the increased production and prices of copra were attributed to the effects of the war; at the same time, though for unexplained reasons, much less Giriama grain was exported than before (Kilifi District Political Records vol. 2).

7. Offical backing for some gerontocracy may have begun in 1910/1911, when, in the second volume of the *Kilifi Political Records,* there is reference to government recognition being given to the "Wanyika" (Mijikenda) "councils of elders". Thereafter references are frequent, often concerning the conflicting obligations of elders to the administration and the people.

8. Some of these "local variations", as he calls them, are well brought out by E. Cotran (1968).

3. The Power of Elders

Tsakani: a Neighbourhood

Kaloleni trading centre stands on the clearly visible edge of the palm belt. To the east palms extend in increasing profusion to the coast. To the west lies arid land of bush and scrub.

Tsakani is one of several clusters of family homesteads dotted around the trading centre. Within the palm belt homesteads are numerous, up to twenty to a square mile, while in the non-palm area of Giriamaland there may be miles between individual homesteads. Tsakani is well within the palm belt and is three miles from the trading centre. Like other homestead clusters in the area, Tsakani was once a cattle-grazing area with only a small population. Immigration and the extension of the palm belt from the 1920s have increased the density of homestead settlement and eliminated the possibility of grazing cattle.

Tsakani has no hard-and-fast boundaries. It is arbitrarily defined and includes twenty-six adjacent homesteads, which I came to know particularly well and in one of which my wife and I lived. There are administrative names for sub-locations, the boundaries of which are clearly defined. But people generally use their own, not administrative, names to describe areas. In the case of Tsakani, which is a fictitious name meaning 'in the forest' in Giriama, there were three terms to refer to some or all of the homesteads in the area. It was not possible to get agreement on the boundaries denoted by these terms, which seemed to express personal notions of spatial inclusion and exclusion of neighbours, as much as anything else. Similarly, the twenty-six homesteads of Tsakani, all the members of which interact frequently, presented themselves to me as something of a neighbourhood. All the homesteads come under the jurisdiction of one of the three sub-chiefs operating in Kaloleni location, and most stand within the official sub-location of Tsakarolovu.

Tsakani occupies an area of about one and one half to two square miles, with a population of 85 men, 124 women, and 213 children living in the twenty-six homesteads. I define the homestead for the moment as no more than an agnatic joint family under a recognised head. On the basis of this definition, the average size of homesteads is just over seven adults (including three men and four women) and eight children. This average is the same as that for Kaloleni location as a whole, according to the tax register.

The main road to Kilifi may be taken to constitute the western boundary of Tsakani. Branching north-east from this road is a smaller one to Chonyi, the sub-location of the Mijikenda sub-group of the same name. This road forms much of the northern boundary of Tsakani. There is another convenient, if again arbitrary, boundary to the south. This is a strip of some few hundred yards of marshland. In other than exceptionally hot weather, most of this is waterlogged and unsuitable for cultivation. At its edges some people grow rice, but otherwise it is unused and uninhabited and stands out in stark contrast to the forest of palms on either side of it.

Running into this marshland, right through the middle of Tsakani from north to south is a small seasonal stream. This never rises to more than a couple of feet during the heavy rains of April and May and becomes a cracked, parched clear-way during the three very hot preceding months from January through March. This small stream is linked to three springs, which have given Tsakani its only claim to fame. Even during the driest period in recall, these springs have never run dry. During the annual hot spell at the beginning of the year, people from nearby neighbourhoods take water from these springs when their own sources have dried up. People in Tsakani are proud of their springs, and they, if anything, might provide a focus of neighbourhood definition, should their supplies of water appear to diminish. But this is a virtual impossibility, and the customary right of all Giriama to use natural springs is not questioned.

The terrain may be said to be typical of the immediate coastal hinterland in that Tsakani is set among rolling hills and dales. Some men say the area has always been well watered. Others claim that before the planting of palms in Tsakani the rainfall was not much higher than farther inland. They believe that the palms brought rain. Whichever is true, all are agreed that it was not until the late 1920s that palms were planted and that until that time the land had been used for cattle-grazing, then the primary form of subsistence. In these respects the area is not different from most other satellite neighbourhoods around Kaloleni trading centre and points to a general process.

From reconstruction of genealogies and the histories given by individual homestead heads, it appears that only three or four homesteads were in Tsakani in the early twenties. To get more precise data than this would be difficult. At a time when claims to land and trees are being made on the basis of right by agnatic ancestry, genealogical accounts are bound to conflict, as indeed they do.

Inheritance and Appropriation

The ecological and demographic changes in Tsakani have made apparent genealogical manoeuvring a frequent feature of claims to land and palms. But the overall legitimacy of agnatic ancestry as the basis of claims is unchallenged. Agnation represents a wide range of potential and actual ties. For instance, property is inherited from father to son. But if sons are too young to administer the property themselves, an agnate of the deceased father acts as guardian for the sons and holds or administers the property in trust for them. If seniority alone were the qualification for effective rights of administration over land and palms, then competing claimants would merely struggle for the title of the most senior agnate. But this may not be enough. A complicating factor is the right of a deceased agnate's widows to choose who should inherit them, regardless of his degree of agnatic closeness to the husband. Such a man may sometimes also act as his deceased "brother's" trustee. As trustee, he may over time appropriate for himself and his own sons property which technically is held in trust for the deceased agnate's sons.

It is clear here that we must distinguish the inheritance of widows from that of property. A man may inherit the widows not only of deceased brothers or agnates of the same generation but also of paternal grandfathers, with the exception of his own biological grandmother. In the few cases of "grandmother" widow inheritance, the deceased grandfather is most often classificatory. More usually widows are inherited by "brothers" of their deceased husbands. In Tsakani sixteen of one hundred four currently married women have been inherited in this way.

Property is inherited from father to son. Ideally, this should follow the demands of the house-property complex. That is to say, if a man has three wives, then his land and trees are divided into three portions, each of which is given over to a uterine sibling group. If the first wife has only one son, the second three, and the third four, then the first wife's son would have by far the largest single plot of land and trees. In such a case elders may advise a more equal distribution of the property, according to the number of sons rather than according to the number of wives.

Mothers attempt, not always effectively, to guard the heritable property of their own sons. This concern appears to be a major motive in a widow's choice of an heir to a deceased husband: a reputedly just man will not abuse his trusteeship and appropriate the property of her sons. A wrong choice may jeopardize her own as well as her sons' future, since it is customary for an aged mother to spend her declining years in a son's homestead. Cautious widows entrust their choice to the advice of sub-clan elders, who may by no means agree easily or quickly on a suitable heir. Different personal obligations and alliances play parts in the arguments preceding a choice.

A guardian who appropriates land when his wards are still young may plant palms and other trees on it. When his wards are old enough to claim their dead father's property, he may claim some or all of it as his own, or beforehand he may have altered the boundaries in his favour. Many land and tree disputes within families stem from this situation.

Ideally, a co-wife's eldest son is the senior of his uterine sibling group. At their father's death, the group is likely to set up residence away from their father's homestead; if their mother is senior co-wife, the group is apt to remain. The senior brother should administer the property and allocate cash proceeds from it. Whether this ideal is observed seems at present a matter of personal expedience.

A prominent Tsakani elder stands outside a traditional oval-shaped house. Most houses nowadays are rectangular and have window openings.

A few brothers have observed the ideal by staying together under their senior. But some have managed to purchase their own land and palms elsewhere, while others have abandoned the property after a quarrel, perhaps regarding it as too little to fight for. Some have set up a homestead separate from a brother, which would entitle them to independent rights over their own share of land and palms, but then have turned instead to working for wages in Mombasa or to tapping palm wine for neighbours. Thus, as with trustee status accompanying widow inheritance, there are a number of situations in which a man may be using land and palms as his own, even though nominally some belongs to agnates.

The Manipulation of Agnation and Clanship

It is clear, then, that through inheritance and appropriation agnatic links may be used as one way of acquiring and holding property. As mentioned, those designated as elders sanction agnatic claims in the government court and in moots, but elders are themselves agnates and have vested interests as such. They have to balance carefully two sets of interests: as a category or group they need to maintain the high value placed on the general principle of agnation; as individuals they need to support whichever claim in any one case supports their own position through genealogical tracing. This might explain the inconsistencies in genealogical accounts by, as well as between, individuals. While many genealogical boundaries are fluid, those of clanship are not: there may be disagreement as to a man's agnatic closeness or seniority in relation to another, but his clan and sub-clan membership are indisputable. Nevertheless, sub-clan ties can be converted into lower-order agnatic links: with the help of witnesses "new" and "closer" agnatic links may be discovered.

In Tsakani twelve clans are represented by the twenty-six homestead heads, thus presenting a picture of considerable clan interspersion at the neighbourhood level. Yet altogether among all 150,000 Giriama there are only twenty-six clans, if by this term we refer to the minimal exogamous group descended unilineally from a mythical ancestor. If we also include wives in Tsakani, most of whom have been married from nearby neighbourhoods, then nearly all the Giriama clans are represented. This does seem to be typical of other Giriama areas. Over the 2,500 square miles of Giriama country, therefore, clans are completely dispersed.

The clans are patrilineal, and there is no evidence of there having ever existed matri-clans, as has been suggested for other Mijikenda sub-groups (Prins 1952). Clans are the exogamous units into which a woman from any other clan, even that of the husband's mother, may be taken in marriage. The possibility of marriage into any clan other than one's own, together with considerable interspersion of clans at the local level, widens the immediate range of choice of spouse. This is a fact of some significance in view of the apparent stability over at least the past half-century in the number of exogamous units, despite a much increased population. A recently published document, written by a district officer who worked among Giriama in 1914, includes the same list of exogamous clans which I was given in the field (Champion 1967). In spite of population increase, therefore, the units of exogamy appear to remain the same.

Ties of neighbourhood are likely to determine which women of eligible clans are married (see Chapter 6). Similarly, though sub-clans, of which there are only two or three to a clan, are the largest units within which widows and property may be inherited, elders claim that it is only within patrilineages of no more than four or five generations that such rights are really awarded. What may happen in practice is for a claimant to translate sub-clan membership into lineage membership. Beyond a couple of generations there is always considerable disagreement as to the genealogy, and, with sufficient support, the claim can be carried. This manipulation is all the more possible in view of the fact that even recognised small lineages are highly dispersed, with the result that memories of precise agnatic links may become hazy in the absence of frequent ties based on common locality.

As an illustration of this lineage dispersion, all the people of Tsakani have at least some grandfather's brothers, father's brothers, and even grandsons, living beyond a range of a hundred miles from Kaloleni. It is not uncommon, therefore, for a senior man to inherit, say, a deceased patrilateral parallel cousin's widow and to have to travel fifty miles or more to his cousin's homestead to consummate the inherited marriage and then return home.

For all these units, from the agnatic joint family through the smallest dispersed lineage, to the sub-clans and clans of Giriama, and beyond even these to each of the Mijikenda sub-groups, the term *mbari* may be used. Thus, in Tsakani, the clan of Mweni is called *mbari,* but so are each of its two constituent sub-clans, Muramba and Maitha. And, at a lower level, two full, half-, or classificatory brothers living together or in their own homesteads are referred to as *mbari.* Again, two neighbouring homestead heads, one of the Muramba and the other of the Maitha sub-clan, refer to each other as *mbari.* Like so many Giriama terms, the diffuseness of reference is an efficient means of enabling the facts of neighbourhood and co-residence to be fitted into an overarching ideology of patriliny. For instance, disputes over land and palms or other trees which occur between homestead heads who are in some way members of the same exogamous clan are discussed and sometimes decided by clan elders *(atumia a mbari),* who may each be variously related through agnation and clanship to the disputants and to each other. Invoking a relationship of *mbari* is thus a useful starting point for mobilising support.

Practically, then, as well as terminologically, clanship and agnation constitute a single range of relationships. I shall henceforth refer to the general principle as that of agnation. The usefulness of *mbari* ties is not necessarily determined by agnatic closeness or seniority but may rest on a reciprocal need for support in claims for property or in domestic or other disputes. A man who is of your *mbari* is thus a potential witness for or against you.

Agnation can be summarised initially as being significant in two main ways. It is a principle by which elders are defined and given authority: decisions regarding eligibility for marriage and inheritance are taken, or sometimes thrashed out, by elders. Agnation is also, of course, the principle by which land, palms, other property, and widows are inherited. But, while heritable rights arc ideally confined to a descent group, the "optative element" open to an individual claimant is high, due to the shallowness of agreed genealogical reckoning.

Other Rights to Property

Agnation represents a range of alternative ways of gaining access to land and palms and to other property. But there are other ways which have nothing to do with agnatic links. Land and palms may be bought outright or may be acquired in mortgage. It is not surprising, therefore, to find that nearly all the homestead heads of Tsakani work land and palms by virtue of a very mixed bag of "rights", many of them contestable. And because they are contestable they strengthen the mediatory role of elders.

A not untypical homestead head may have some land and/or palms which he inherited from his father, some which he may have bought or taken in mortgage, and some which he holds in trust, say, for a brother's sons or for some of his own younger brothers. Even more complicated is the situation in which he or his father may have planted palms during the early settlement period of Tsakani on land which belonged to a family of a different clan which originally allowed him or his father to farm annual crops there. Both the court and the moots rule that in this case the palms belong to the family which planted them, and the land belongs to the original family.

This latter complexity has been brought about by the extension of the palm belt. The government court has recognised the difficulty, and nowadays it is illegal for a man to plant trees of any kind on land over which he or his clan can be shown to have no more than rights of use. The government court will actually order a man who has done this in recent years on, for example, land which he was allowed to use for subsistence cultivation, to uproot the palms or other trees which he has planted, provided that they are still young. Should they be mature, he will be obliged to sell them to whoever owns the land or to reach some settlement as to their use.

From life histories it is clear that in the twenties and early thirties in Tsakani and other former cattle-grazing, mixed-farming areas of Kaloleni, people of quite different clans, many of whom were related matrilaterally or affinally, would be allowed to live on and cultivate what was then much more plentiful land. These tenants-at-will would plant a few palms for wine. This would not then have been seen by the owners—if they saw it at all—as a possible reason for disputation in the future.

But, as explained, immigration and an increased density of population, together with a vastly greater use of land for growing palms, have resulted in land scarcity. Claims to old, but now profitable, family or clan land are being made years after a family has left it. Non-agnates may be persuaded to leave the land or, if this fails, may be accused of being in unlawful occupation: they are "discovered" to have built their homesteads there without permission and to have planted palms on the land years previously without the consent of a senior member of a family. These claims are being made by younger members of families, after the deaths of their fathers when they are taking stock of what family resources there are to be divided among themselves and their brothers.

All these factors illustrate three related features of contemporary Giriama society as it operates in Tsakani. One is a tendency to revive agnatic rights to property or residence in an area. This is an instance of a more general phenomenon found in other parts of the world. Meggitt (1965) shows that among the Mae-Enga of New Guinea competition for scarce land restricts to agnates the range of persons eligible to use it. In East Nepal Caplan (1970, p. 54) describes how, in response to Hindu economic and political pressure, the range among a "tribal" people is limited specifically to those regarded as true agnates. In Tsakani, the claims number among many already described which justify the mediatory role of Giriama elders.

This second feature can be summarised as being a constant need for sympathetic witnesses: whether reviving claims to old family land or acquiring or disposing of property, a man needs witnesses to confirm his rights of tenure or, as with pledge and mortgage, redemption, or that he has disposed of trust property for legitimate reasons.

A third feature is the strengthened power of senior members of a family. Whether or not there is written evidence of rights in property, as there has been in some transactions since World War II, older witnesses are regarded by the government court and moots as generally the most qualified to testify in claims. They may be witnesses for other families in one context, but in another they may themselves be claimants. As older men they have a definite advantage over most younger men. The *sine qua non* of the status of witness is to be a homestead head, though not all heads are witnesses.

In Tsakani, indeed, it is possible to speak of a rough, two-fold ranking of homestead heads as regards their reputations as witnesses. The most sought-after witnesses are likely to be in the upper age bracket of homestead heads. They are likely to be regularly represented on clan and neighbourhood moots and to be invited to give evidence in the government court in the Kaloleni District compound. The most eminent will be active members of an important politico-welfare organisation called the Mijikenda Union (referred to in Chapter 8). Finally, as an ultimate seal of legitimacy on their status, they will be recognised to have ritual expertise: as neighbourhood doctors administering traditional medicine and as spokesmen on esoteric elements of Giriama ritual life.

One of the most obvious outward marks of such seniority is the uncontested right of elders (men over fifty, at least) to carry the plaited bag of medicines known as *mukoba*. A traditional doctor is known as *muganga wa mukoba,* as distinct from other ritual specialists. Neither women nor younger men carry such bags. Furthermore, basket-weaving is a leisure occupation which is the preserve of elders, to the exclusion of young homestead heads, however economically successful. There is thus a basic homology of age, medicines, and basket-making/carrying as to youth, lack of medicines, and no basket-making/carrying.

It is the most prominent elders whose support is so valuable to enterprising farmers, who are themselves homestead heads but who are likely to be classed as young and ignorant of customary law and ritual. I now introduce the homestead heads of Tsakani in the light of these congruent differences of age and ritual and economic power.

Witnesses and the Power of Age

I have until now spoken of twenty-six family homesteads in Tsakani, implying that each has only one homestead head. In following the Giriama term for homestead head *(mwenye mudzi),* this is so. Giriama will say that a homestead can have only one head. It is possible, however, to isolate objective criteria for defining the position. A head receives and redistributes cash from the sale of the produce of crops, palms, and other trees held by himself or on behalf of members of his homestead. He is the spokesman for the homestead in matters affecting the use, disposal, or transfer of rights in the property. He is responsible for organising the marriages of homestead members and for making sure that bridewealth for males is found from the homestead's resources. He is also the chief ritual representative at funerals and other ceremonies concerning people of the homestead, and at séances, oracles, or ordeals performed on behalf of members of his homestead.

As such, the homestead head exhibits the classical multiplicity and mutual reinforcement of political, jural, economic, and ritual roles frequently ascribed to members of small-scale, technologically rudimentary societies. But since homesteads in Tsakani are small, averaging just over three men, four women, and eight children, the combined authority of these roles operates within a limited domestic sphere. Homesteads rarely include non-agnates. They generally comprise married sons, sometimes junior unmarried brothers, and, in only eleven instances, married brothers of the head. Inheriting widows and acting as their sons' guardians is, of course, one way in which this domestic authority may be extended. Otherwise, a homestead head must achieve extensions of personal influence by becoming a respected clan and neighbourhood elder and perhaps even being represented on government court panels or in the Mijikenda Union.

Using the objective criteria outlined, twenty-four of the twenty-six homesteads have, in fact, no more than one head, thus giving empirical substance to the Giriama concept of *mwenye mudzi.* But one homestead has two senior members each of whom administers his property independently. Another exceptionally large homestead, consisting of twenty-one adults and forty-one children, has four sub-family heads who continue to live in the same homestead but who administer their property independently. In both homesteads there is a nominal or customary head who is referred to as *mwenye mudzi* and who still represents the whole

Contrasting leisure pursuits of young and old in Tsakani: while elders weave baskets, the younger men make music. The elder at the left is a neighborhood doctor.

homestead at neighbourhood ceremonies. The strains of fission are there, however. A scarcity of land for further homestead settlement in Tsakani and a concern by the sub-family heads that their palms will be unprotected if they move farther away, appear to hold the strains in abeyance. The customary holder of the title *mwenye mudzi* remains unchallenged. For the moment, I treat these two homesteads as having only the one customary head because I wish to illustrate the empirical context in which the customary notion of homestead head or *mwenye mudzi* is set.

The sample of twenty-six homestead heads is too small to show any more than suggestive correlations between age, size of homestead, and ritual and economic status. The tables presented in this book, together with the individual cases, are meant to be descriptive of Tsakani as a neighbourhood. There are the usual, but statistically unverifiable, impressions from other areas of Kaloleni that Tsakani is not untypical.

Much of a head's influence is said by Giriama to rest on the size of his homestead. They explain that a man who is able to "rule" many people must have qualities which qualify him for leadership in other spheres also. How much of a Giriama ideal is this? Seven of the eleven largest homesteads in Tsakani are indeed headed by men who are over fifty, while ten of the fifteen smallest have heads who are under fifty. But there are a few young men heading large homesteads and older men heading small ones (see Tables 1 and 2).

TABLE 1. RELATIONSHIP BETWEEN SIZE OF HOMESTEAD AND
AGE OF HEAD (Mwenye Mudzi) IN TSAKANI.

age of head	homesteads of up to 15 persons	homesteads of more than 15 persons	total
up to 50	10 (38.4%)	4 (15.4%)	14 (53.8%)
over 50	5 (19.3%)	7 (26.9%)	12 (46.2%)
TOTAL	15 (57.7%)	11 (42.3%)	26

TABLE 2. AGES OF HOMESTEAD HEADS IN TSAKANI.

age groups	17–19	20–29	30–39	40–49	50–59	60–69	70–79	TOTAL
number of adult males	6(7%)	27(31.8%)	21(24.7%)	10(11.8%)	14(16.4%)	6(7%)	1(1.2%)	85(99.9%)
number of homestead heads	0	3	6	5	6	5	1	26
percentage of all homestead heads	0	11.5%	23.1%	19.2%	23.1%	19.2%	3.8%	99.9%
percentage of adult males in own age group	0	11.1%	28.6%	50%	42.8%	83.3%	100%	———

An extreme example is of a young man under twenty-nine who has seventeen adults and children in his homestead. He was only about eighteen when his father died and, since none of his father's brothers or agnates of his own generation lived with him, would by custom have been expected to move to the home of the "brother" who inherited his mother. However, he considered that he had the strength and wisdom to manage his father's estate and homestead independently and, after successfully lobbying for the support of a selected group of elders, decided to do so. He has certainly prospered in the eleven years since his father died. He has married off two sisters, has planted palms, has bought a few cattle, which are pastured in another area, and now has two wives and a number of children. He stands in striking contrast to a neighbouring head of over seventy who has failed to gather around him a large family, in spite of having been head for forty-nine years. This man has two married daughters living at their husbands' homes, but only one married son. Many of the children he produced died, while his son has begotten only one child with his two wives, one of whom has been with him for twenty-eight years.

The Giriama ideal that an older head should have a larger homestead than a younger one and that a head should not be particularly young anyway, is thus not infrequently flouted by natural misfortune, as well as by men's own endeavours. But seniority continues to confer many rights, privileges, and recognised ritual and judicial powers, and few young heads, however enterprising or prosperous by local standards, are able to ignore this fact. Men between twenty and twenty-nine years of age are the most numerous of the eighty-five Tsakani men, but that age group provides by far the fewest homestead heads. It is from about forty and fifty onward that a man's chances of being a head seem to increase markedly. By the time he is sixty, he is almost certain to head a homestead (see Table 2).

That the government court, the district administration, and the chief and sub-chiefs look to older homestead heads as being likely to provide the most reliable testimony in disputes and claims over property is based on a reasonable assumption and is not simply because custom dictates so. Since World War II, claims to land and palms in Tsakani have increased both in number and intensity. To be able to speak as an original settler in the neighbourhood in the days when only cattle were grazed there or as the proven son, or even grandson, of a settler, is an advantageous starting point in any contested claims for rights in property. Men can use their seniority to their own advantage, or it may be so used by others.

Half the heads in Tsakani have held this position for fewer than ten years, but more than half the homesteads themselves have been established on their present sites for at least twenty years (see Table 3). This anchoring of family homesteads

TABLE 3. TENURE OF HOMESTEAD HEADS IN TSAKANI.

years homestead has been on present site	number of heads with less than 10 years' tenure	number of heads with 10 or more years' tenure	TOTAL
less than 20	8 (30.8%)	3 (11.5%)	11 (42.3%)
more than 20	5 (19.3%)	10 (38.4%)	15 (57.7%)
TOTAL	13 (50.1%)	13 (49.8%)	26

contrasts with a more mobile pattern before palms were planted in profusion, thus obliging people to protect their property by settling permanently.

As well as supposedly having the longest memories as witnesses, then, the older homestead heads in Tsakani constitute the long-established core of a stable population. The rate of immigration into the neighbourhood has had to slow because of land scarcity, and few families who have moved into Tsakani during the last twenty-five years have left it. As senior members of this increasingly stable community, the wintesses have come to represent the vested interests of many people other than themselves.

However, in coming to represent so many vested interests, the witnesses are supporting two logically contradictory principles, that of agnation and that of individual contract. They are brought in to mediate on property claims based on agnatic ancestry. As discussed fu!ly in the previous section, their collective status as mediators depends on continued use of agnation and clanship for allocating property and organising marriage. Yet, simply because they *are* recognised as legitimate witnesses by the government court, local moots, and ordinary people, they are also asked to testify to transactions of land and palms which make no reference to agnatic relatedness and clanship, but which are based on sale or mortgage.

All homestead heads make use of both principles, according to context: they inherit property and invoke agnatic claims, but they also buy if possible and sell if necessary. But an underlying cleavage is developing in Tsakani, which becomes clearer when viewed over a period of time which is longer than and which spans individual situations. The cleavage is between those people who increasingly rely on and benefit by contract and those who are limited to acquiring property through agnation.

This cleavage is not, however, between clearly delineated classes. With one exception, the differences of wealth among people in Tsakani are not great. Life styles remain broadly similar. There is essentially no more than an embryonic development of divisions between rich and poor. Despite emerging property differences, people share a common belief in two central aspects of Giriama ritual and custom. One is the power of medicines which may be present both in ritual therapy, or the beneficial use of traditional medicines, and in its obverse, sorcery, or the evil use of medicines. The other is the power of sanctions centering on notions of honour and shame. Paradoxically, it is this sharing of common beliefs which is helping to accelerate divisions of wealth among the people. It is to the present distribution of wealth among Tsakani heads that I now turn. I want to show how the polarity of age and youth is seen to be homologous with that of ritual and economic prowess.

4. The Polarization of Custom and Contract

Economic Managers

I have dealt so far with twenty-six homestead heads, defined traditionally by the term *mwenye mudzi*. Following the objective economic criteria I have outlined, it is possible to view two of the homesteads as having more than one head —one with two and the second with four. In each case, the men live together and in ritual matters acknowledge one as the principle figure, although each administers his land and palms separately. These are instances of ritual roles not buttressing economic ones, but of the two operating independently of each other. These and other manifestly ritual roles among Giriama seem at first to be compensatory (see Southall, 1954, p. 95, and Turner 1957, p. 316). That is to say, people acknowledge the ritual leadership of others, provided that this does not deprive them of the right to administer their own economic affairs independently. Yet, such roles are more than compensatory. They also have a crucially important ambivalence. In their cultural expression, they may be said to hide contradictory principles of organization.

There are, then, thirty independent "economic managers" in Tsakani, of whom twenty-six are known by the customary title of *mwenye mudzi* ('homestead head'). Giriama are perfectly aware that their society has undergone rapid economic change over the past twenty-five years. They like to talk about men who have expanded their holdings of palms and will provide stories of their careers which are usually biased or discrepant, but from which some consistencies nevertheless emerge. A universal comment is that those men who have accumulated many palms and are now rich are "young", by which is meant that such men are of about middle age. How idealised is this correlation between youth and wealth, and what is the nature of this wealth which people evaluate?

Coconut palms are the most common and most important economically productive asset.[1] In order to simplify, I have used them alone for assessing wealth differences. From the Giriama viewpoint, too, palms are symbolically, as well as economically, valued: they provide the palm wine, which connotes sharing; the copra, which is the prime cash crop; and even food, in the form of the flesh of unmatured coconuts.

Coconut palms are durable wealth in so far as they have very long lives—well over fifty years, in most cases. Most palms in Tsakani have been planted within the past quarter-century, and many are much fewer than twenty years old. Age is taken into account in evaluating a field of palms, but an agreed price for the purchase of a single palm is nowadays twenty shillings (one East African shilling = 14 cents, U.S., in 1966, or 4.3 pence sterling). There is no set sum for mortgaging or pledging palms, though it is in all cases less than twenty shillings and is determined by such factors as the length of the mortgage and the specific relationship of the two parties to the transaction. Kin, for example, expect and sometimes get favourable treatment if they need money to pay off debts or to meet emergencies.

From the point of view of the government tax assessors, twenty shillings is also the amount which a coconut palm may reasonably be expected to yield in a year through the sale of coconuts and copra. Palms which are tapped for wine are reckoned by the assessors to bring in one hundred fifty shillings a year. But this takes no account of labour costs, nor of the fact that the life of a palm's fruitfulness is shortened by tapping. In Tsakani the twenty shillings expected yield is probably higher than the actual yield, according to my investigations, though much depends on the farmer's competence. It is difficult to assess whether a man actually earns one hundred fifty shillings from owning a palm which is tapped. Since most homesteads have only a few palms under tap and approximately equal each other in the number tapped, it is possible, for comparison, to ignore the yield from tapping and to regard twenty shillings for each palm as indicating both its transferable wealth and its yearly income. This represents a quick return on the initial purchase capital. I also ignore the fact that a small proportion of the "palms" converted into cash value in Table 4 are citrus and cashew-nut trees, each of which is sold for fifteen shillings and is assessed for tax purposes at this sum. The proportion of these trees is small, and it seems pointless to complicate matters by singling them out for special attention.

Having established what constitutes wealth, both in an objective sense and in the view of Giriama themselves, let us now ask whether the Giriama notion that youth goes with wealth is borne out by the facts. As with the correlation between age and size of homestead, we can see from Table 4 that there is some substance in this idea. Of the poorer economic managers, rather more are over fifty years of age, while, conversely, more of the wealthier managers are less than fifty.

TABLE 4. VALUE OF PALMS OWNED BY YOUNG AND BY
OLD ECONOMIC MANAGERS OF TSAKANI.

value of palms as transferable wealth/annual income	number of managers of up to 50 years of age	number of managers of more than 50 years of age	TOTAL
up to 3,000 shillings	8 (26.7%)	12 (40%)	20 (66.7%)
more than 3,000 shillings	7 (23.3%)	3 (10%)	10 (33.3%)
TOTAL	15 (50%)	15 (50%)	30

Looking beyond the table for further details, we have eighteen managers controlling palms whose cash value is less than 2,000 shillings but more than 1,000 shillings and fourteen whose property is actually worth less than 1,000 shillings —in six cases amounting to almost nothing. Higher up the scale, past the 3,000-shilling mark and among the remaining ten managers, are four whose assets exceed 7,000 shillings—in two cases well above this. Three are in their thirties and one in his forties.

Three of these four wealthiest men are entrepreneurs in the fullest sense of the word: they continue to amass palms, but have also branched out into commerce. One owns a truck and plies a healthy trade between Mombasa and Kaloleni collecting oranges, bananas, and other specially grown fruits for sale in the main Mombasa market of Mwembe Tayari. The second owns two shops and a tractor and plough, which he hires out to enterprising farmers with land outside the palm belt.The third specialises in growing maize, for which he has built large permanent stores, which were very expensive but which enable him to hoard the maize until times of the year when supplies are low and prices high. In other words, he has exploited an environmental "niche", to use Barth's term (1963, p.9). This is that palms take up much of the land that might otherwise be used for growing maize for subsistence. Most families run out of maize before the next harvest, but, through the dependable and therefore regular sale of copra and sometimes of fruit, usually have enough cash to buy maize for subsistence. They can buy maize flour packeted from any shop, but the Tsakani entrepreneur is able to provide maize on the cob, which can be ground into fresher and cheaper flour.

The Economic Context of Intergenerational Relations.

These three entrepreneurs are prime examples of what witnesses or elders claim is a reversal of traditional values: namely that young men should not head homesteads or manage their own affairs independently and should not, therefore, be men of wealth. In general, however, young men are subject to effective economic sanctions. Looked at another way, this polarity of adjacent generations within families can be seen as a conflict of opposed categories competing for the same sources of wealth. This is most obvious in the use of land and palms and in the expectation that a father or guardian will provide a man with his bride-wealth.

Proportionally few young men in Tsakani less than thirty years of age are economic managers. They constitute 39 percent of Tsakani's adult male population of eighty-five, but provide only 10 percent of the thirty managers. The difference between these proportions is narrowed but still significantly wide for men under forty, who are more than 63 percent of Tsakani's adult males but who provide only 33 percent of the managers. The narrowing continues with men under fifty, who number 75 percent of Tsakani men and 50 percent of the managers. For men over fifty the ratios are reversed, so proportionally more of them are managers: they are only about 25 percent of all the men, but include 50 percent of the managers.

An enterprising farmer poses beside his newly built granary, in which he stores maize until times when supplies are low and prices high. The construction is of stone and mortar on concrete foundations and, as can be seen, required considerable excavation.

33

What is it that prevents more young men from insisting on setting up their own homesteads or managing their own affairs independently of fathers or guardians? Apart from deterrents of a personal or moral nature, there is a possible economic disadvantage in striking out from a parental homestead while still young. This is that a young, independent homestead head is unlikely to have male members in his homestead who can look after his wife (or wives) and family while he himself works in Mombasa or some other fairly distant town or trading centre. By continuing to live in a homestead headed by a father, father's brother, or elder brother, he can at least migrate to work and leave his family in their care, even though there may sometimes be friction between relatives within the homestead. Twenty-two (nearly 50 percent) of the fifty-five young men who are not yet economic managers, but most of whom are married, are able to do this. A general scarcity of wage-employment prevents others from doing so, but does not prevent them from hanging on in the hope of jobs' becoming available.

It thus follows that economic managers have normally relinquished any wage-employment they may have had. Of those who have worked in the past, all gave up their jobs immediately upon becoming heads. From life histories in Tsakani and elsewhere in Kaloleni, it is clear that this is an established pattern. A new homestead head ceases to work in a full-time job, especially one which requires him to live away from home. Few have any more than low-paid jobs, so it is as much, if not more, profitable to take up the headship and so obtain full rights of administration over the family's land and palms. More importantly, the family property now has to be protected from rival claims or encroachment. In summary, then, economic managers tend not to combine farming with wage-employment which requires them to live away from home. The few exceptions to this are those men whose education and skills qualify them for jobs providing wages sufficiently high for them to employ other men to protect and work their farms on their behalf. Only a couple of men are in a position to do this in Tsakani, and there are very few in Kaloleni.

Sixty percent of Tsakani men are exclusively agricultural workers. They include economic managers and younger men who are unable to find wage-employment. The rest combine farming with some form of wage-employment, either in or around Kaloleni trading centre or in one of the coastal towns. They are usually junior members of a homestead—typically, sons, nephews, or younger brothers. With only four of these men in clerical or skilled jobs, the money coming into a homestead from wage-labour is not usually very much, but it at least constitutes a contribution to subsistence demands.

While it is useful for this reason to have some members of a homestead in wage-employment, it is recognised that the money so earned is subject to different claims than the income from the produce of land and palms. Giriama say that wage-earnings are acquired "by a man's own sweat" and recognise the right of the earner to spend it more or less as he pleases, provided that immediate obligations to his family are not shirked.

Later I shall focus on the question of how men acquire the money to buy palms and land. Wage-income may be an initial useful source of such capital, but three factors work against it's becoming a primary source of capital accumulation. One is that wage-employment has become increasingly scarce, not only in Mombasa and other coastal centres but throughout Kenya. The second is the simple fact that most jobs undertaken are unskilled and low-paid and so allow only a negligible rate of saving, if any. The third is the fact that, since most wage-earners are junior members of homesteads, they are not in a position to buy palms or land other than through the authority of their fathers or guardians. To disregard a father's authority is impracticable, since it would involve setting up an independent homestead, which, as mentioned, is incompatible with wage-employment. A few sons have helped their fathers to buy palms, but many are reluctant to do this for fear that at the father's death others of his sons will not recognise the wage-earner's early contribution to the inheritance. Answers to questions on income expenditure are apt to be unreliable, but from observation there is little reason to doubt young wage-earners' assertions that they tend to spend their money on food, clothes, and "luxurious things" (which are clearly rare, but may include wrist-watches, very occasionally cheap transistor radios, and trinkets and clothes for wives).

The tendency for wage-earnings to be used more for subsistence and consumer articles than as direct capital for purchasing palms is thus partly a result of paternal control, which it also serves to entrench. In this connection, it is interesting to observe that even when they are in wage-employment, sons rarely contribute cash to their own bridewealth for a first wife. There is the customary expectation that a father or guardian will provide bridewealth for his son or ward. This is not simply an ideal obligation as it is among some other peoples of Kenya, but it has actually been complied with in all but one of about forty cases in Tsakani over the past ten years, even for men whose earnings are above average. Just as a man is reluctant to help a father buy palms for fear that it may be "eaten up" when brothers take their shares of the inheritance, so he is reluctant to provide his own bridewealth and effectively cede his share of the family property normally due to him from the marriage of a sister. Brotherly love does not always surmount competition for patrimony.

Bridewealth among all Mijikenda, except Digo, is considerable, amounting in Tsakani to a cash average over the past five years of 1,425 shillings. Because sons do not contribute to their own bridewealth and because, anyway, few are likely to have made much money from wage-employment, the need for bridewealth strengthens sons' dependence on fathers and in turn endorses the authority of the latter. This is aptly illustrated by the fact that the hard bargaining accompanying bridewealth negotiations is between the fathers of the prospective groom and bride. The bride and groom have usually courted and chosen each other beforehand, but they refer all negotiable matters to their fathers.

This economic dependence by sons or wards on their fathers or guardians would surely diminish should considerable wage-earning opportunities present themselves. In their absence, fathers continue to control the use of patrimonial property and effectively restrict sons' opportunities for acquiring palms or land independently. These economic factors, then, provide an empirical context for Giriama notions of the polarity of adjacent generations. The broad cultural expression of intergenerational relations obviously predates these particular factors and, in a variety of forms, is an underlying feature of all societies.

Among Giriama the precise modern economic context is pointed up by specific crisis situations: a father who is a poor economic manager and who appears to have squandered property belonging to his family may suffer the acrimony of sons who are therefore unable to marry; guardians who have squandered or deviously appropriated young men's rightful bridewealth are inevitably depicted as the wicked uncles characteristic of societies with fraternal succession (only a few guardians are brothers or agnates of the same generation); sons and nephew are denied easy access to land and palms. The conflict of adjacent generations is thus not only expressed popularly at the level of complaint or sorrow, but is seen to be supported by empirical instances.

In Tsakani it is only by becoming a homestead head or economic manager that a younger man can even begin to increase his economic stakes. And as explained, this striking out for independence cannot easily be done before the death of a father or guardian.

From the figures given earlier, it is clear that the older homestead heads are correct in claiming that the three young entrepreneurs of Tsakani have reversed the "value" that age and economic control should go together. Helped initially by no less a fact of nature than the death of a father, each of these three has thereafter successfully exploited his own environmental niche. There are other young economic managers who, as we saw, also have above-average wealth.

Since variations in the control of economic resources roughly follow stages of a family's life cycle, we might expect that the property accumulated by these younger managers, regardless of their early start, would eventually be divided by their sons as patrimony. If there were many sons, this would result in small shares for each and would thwart the development of even relatively large, property-owning family dynasties. This will undoubtedly happen to the property accumulated by some of these younger managers. But it is a problem well understood by Giriama. With the exception of a few men in Kaloleni, they do not respond by restricting the number of their sons by having fewer wives. Instead, they attempt explicitly to accumulate sufficiently large holdings of palms and land to remain economically viable as capital-producing enterprises even after their division through inheritance. Enterprising farmers frankly state the problem and their proposed solution, and it is this recognition which underlies the scramble for palms in Tsakani and Kaloleni during the past twenty-five years. And this is what has caused palm ownership increasingly to be concentrated in the hands of a minority in Tsakani.

The Ritual Community

Although emerging economic differences among managers are conceptualised as a reversal of the normal expectation that age and economic control will go together, it can be argued that all Giriama share certain key cosmological assumptions. It must be remembered that I am dealing with innovators who were born and brought up *within* the community in which they operate. As a result, perhaps, of the effects of socialization in that community and of continuing involvement in a system of social relations, men interact frequently with each other on the basis of a number of common assumptions regarding the mystical order of supplication and blame. That is to say, they share ideas of how best to divine, diagnose, and rectify misfortune by mystical means. They are members of a single "community of suffering", to use Turner's phrase (1957, p. *xxi*).

It may be technically impossible to provide proper evidence that all members of a community believe in the practice and efficacy of, say, sorcery. It is possible, however, to observe people making use of the concrete cultural apparatus supporting sorcery beliefs namely, the techniques of divination and curing—and responding to the demands transmitted by these techniques. All men and women in Tsakani have at some time made use of these techniques. They thereby demonstrate their belief in sorcery and mystical cure. From the more usual impressionistic viewpoint, also, the genuine concern for and interest in such mystical forces is universal in Kaloleni.

In other words, all Giriama men, regardless of their economic status, need ritual practitioners who can divine and cure. The young entrepreneurs and other enterprising managers in Tsakani see themselves and are seen by others to be especially susceptible to the malevolence of jealous relatives and neighbours. The assumption seems to be widespread in Africa that economically successful persons are likely to suffer the sorcery or witchcraft of those who feel relatively deprived. During 1966 and 1967 ministers of the independent Kenya government considered the intense belief in sorcery among Mijikenda to be hindering economic development in the area and made the "perils" of the belief a main topic of their political rallies. Incipient entrepreneurs who are themselves believers are undoubtedly faced by the threat of sorcery and, even if they are not deterred from pursuing expansionist economic aims, must adopt strategies to cope with it.

Like other men and women, the three entrepreneurs in Tsakani make use of local diviners and traditional doctors. In this way they are part of the ritual community. Who, then, are the doctors and diviners, and in what special way is the problem of the entrepreneur as an innovator or deviant dealt with in the cosmological system?

The Ritual Experts

It may be no surprise at this point to introduce as the traditional doctors in Tsakani certain of the most venerable and influential homestead heads. Only homestead heads may be accredited neighbourhood doctors. Of the twenty-six heads in Tsakani, four are doctors. What is significant for this analysis is the fact that they are all over fifty years of age—that is, in the upper age bracket—and that none of them has many palms. One does have a little more than 2,000 shillings' worth and so is just above the Tsakani average, but the other three have less than this—in two cases, less than 1,000 shillings' worth.

There is thus a suggestion of an homology of ritual prowess and economic success with age and youth among homestead heads. This is not only suggested by the figures relating to Tsakani, but also by a sample of twenty neighbourhood doctors in areas adjacent to Tsakani.

What is perhaps more interesting is that most of these doctors established and developed their practices at a point in their lives when they may reasonably be said to have missed any chance of expanding their land and palms: their daughters were by then all married, so that no more bridewealth was due in the homestead; they would no longer migrate for wage-labour; and they had insufficient palms to accumulate capital from the income they produced.

Nearly all of them have become neighbourhood doctors within the past ten years. During this period, they claim to have bought the knowledge, medicines, spells, charms, and specially constructed gourds and baskets needed for their work. These items might cost hundreds of shillings. But, unlike the purchase of palms, this expenditure is spread out over the years, so that, to these men, medical practice presented a lesser but useful alternative investment. The most difficult problem in becoming established is to become "introduced" to an established doctor who can sell the knowledge with the medicines and other tools of the trade and who, in the name of his own reputation, will vouch for the new doctor's credentials.

It should not be doubted that sums of money *are* transacted for medicines. The process of becoming a neighbourhood doctor is, however, more gradual and informal than this affirmation of status implies. Any older homestead head, or *mwenye mudzi,* is by definition able to effect certain curses and cures with respect to his own immediate family: these are powers which he can claim have been handed down to him by this father and which, provided his familial authority is strong, can be seen to be effective at least within his own family. But to extend this ritual influence to the neighbourhood requires an introduction. Introductions are effected by and between men who are not, at that time, competing for the same patients. They tend, therefore, to be from nearby but separate neighbourhoods. Sometimes a man may be fortunate enough to make contact with a well known Muslim doctor in, say, Mombasa.

Relations between new and established doctors are not, however, formalised, nor are they necessarily enduring. Once he is established, the new doctor may compete with his former sponsor. As in all professions, there is competition within the ranks, which may nevertheless close when the profession itself seems threatened. It is hard to maintain a consistently high rate of success in Giriama medical practice. Genuine skills are required in such things as having a supply of the right herbs and administering the correct dosage: a little more than the correct dosage may turn a sound purgative into a lethal poison.[2] The well presented dramatic and ceremonial aspects of one man's medical practice may win additional custom. Exceptionally skilled men become national figures, of whom Kabwere of Malindi is surely the most notable among Giriama. By contrast, many neighbourhood doctors see a sorry and premature end to their careers.

The competition between neighbourhood doctors is not naked. Each has his own remedy for a particular ailment or misfortune, which he will apply when approached, but he will not approach the patients of another doctor. His medical practice is advertised more subtly than this, through his reputation, as spread by friends and satisfied clients. Naked competition must be avoided, because the doctors and other older homestead heads have a common interest in maintaining their status as witnesses at an informal level as well as in local moots and in the government court.

Two of the four Tsakani doctors are additionally important members of the Kaloleni branch of the Mijikenda Union, which arbitrates informally in many disputes. For many years since its inception in 1945, its members have been called on by the colonial and later the independent government administration to sound out and represent the views of the ordinary people. Like individual members of the Mijikenda Union who settle cases, neighbourhood doctors expect no less than two shillings for their services at any one session. The monthly income of the four Tsakani doctors ranged between forty and sixty shillings, of which a few shillings would ordinarily be used for the purchase of medicines. A few doctors in Kaloleni earn more than this.

It must be emphasised that these doctors practice only traditional medicine. There are also two or three employees of the Kaloleni hospital who privately offer penicillin injections and first-aid service at their homes outside of working hours. These are relatively young men whose skills are recognised as being appropriate to certain physical problems. But they do not claim to be able to treat illness for which a mystical cause has been divined. Similarly, the services of the hospital in Kaloleni are used either in conjunction with traditional medicine, as a last resort, or for "understandable" reasons like child-bearing (most Giriama women questioned stated that they preferred to have a hospital delivery). As in many parts of Africa, the legitimacy of Giriama traditional medicine rests on the belief that there are certain afflictions which are best, or even only, assuaged by the use of herbs, roots, and other medicines administered in the mystical idiom of charms, spells, and ritualistic performance. Afflicted people may in reality switch between use of "European" and Giriama medicines, but this does not appear to undermine the legitimacy of the latter.

The Use of External Ritual

Increased wealth in Kaloleni over at least the past twenty-five years appears to have had two consequences. One is an increase in the number of homestead heads who have become neighbourhood doctors.[3] This has clearly given an extra edge to the competition among them for clientele. A second consequence, therefore, is an openly stated claim by doctors to have bought charms, spells, medicines, and styles of performance from Muslim Swahili doctors residing in Mombasa or Malindi and to have thereby increased their repertoires of skills. They claim that their repertoires consist predominantly of traditional Giriama items, but that they may top them up, so to speak, with Islamic items.

It will be remembered that for many generations Giriama have resisted conversion to Islam—or Christianity, for that matter—and so have retained the cultural exclusiveness on which their changing modes of economic self-sufficiency have depended. Giriama doctors do not, therefore, normally become Muslim, even though the power of Islamic medicines for good and for evil is often recognised as supreme. They strike a nice balance by remaining non-Muslim but supplementing their skills with purchased Islamic ritual power. Scarcity represents value, and the most astute doctors claim that they need to use this Islamic power only infrequently. The four Tsakani doctors fall into this category.

It is interesting, therefore, that the three entrepreneurs and a fourth wealthy farmer, whose assets exceed 7,000 shillings, are Muslim. At first sight this would seem to place the entrepreneurs, the wealthiest men in Tsakani, in a ritual category similar to that of the doctors. And yet I have been arguing that the doctors, as poor men of some seniority excercising judicial and ritual influence, stand opposed to the young entrepreneurs. This is certainly the case. It is also true that both sets make use of Islam, but they do so by different methods and for different reasons.

Giriama Muslims are of two types. First are those who are the children or grandchildren of converted Muslims. They are thus born into Islam. Though they may not always attend a mosque, pray five times a day, give alms, or expect to make a pilgrimage to Mecca, they always fast during Ramadhan and observe Islamic commensal obligations. They will not eat the meat of beasts which have not been slaughtered by Muslims, nor will they drink alcohol—not even the palm wine which is of symbolic significance for Giriama. Frequently they will choose to marry other Giriama or Mijikenda Muslims. They show signs, therefore, of constituting a corporate grouping within Giriama society. But they still follow the rules of Giriama clan exogamy and remain members of specific sub-clans, and they will refer to themselves by both their Muslim and Giriama clan and other names. As elders they will settle cases and sit on government court panels like other Giriama elders. Their fathers or grandfathers will have moved to Kaloleni from coastal areas where Muslims, mostly non-Giriama, predominate and for many generations have been economically and politically dominant.

Second are those whom I have elsewhere called therapeutic Muslims (Parkin 1970). These are men (and women) who were born of non-Muslim Giriama parents. They have become possessed by spirits which are judged by a diviner to be of Islamic origin, to be powerful, and to be likely to cause the possessed person's illness, and even death, unless they are appeased. In order to appease the

Islamic spirit(s) the afflicted person is told by the diviner that he must "become" Muslim. He, too, is not required to pray, give alms, go to Mecca, or attend a mosque. He may already be married to a non-Muslim woman and will continue to marry non-Muslims, though his wife or wives may well discard the traditional Giriama topless cotton skirt for a Muslim wrap or European dress. He must, however, observe the fast of Ramadhan and at all times abstain from eating "unclean" meat, from drinking alcohol, and from using certain traditional Giriama cooking utensils and sometimes even ordinary Giriama foods. Commensal restrictions are therefore introduced into relations between these afflicted persons and the rest of the non-Muslim community.

There are a little more than 450 Giriama homestead heads living fully within the palm belt in Kaloleni location. Only 27 (6 percent) are Muslims, most of them of the first type, born of a Muslim father. All have assets in the form of palms and land which are well above the average. Of the four Muslim heads in Tsakani, including the three entrepreneurs and the wealthy farmer, two (both entrepreneurs) are therapeutic Muslims and two, born Muslims. Let me focus on the institution of therapeutic Islam, which appears to be a reflex of the economic changes of the past twenty-five years in Kaloleni, though it seems to have operated as a possible initial stage in a process of conversion at different times in other Mijikenda areas. For instance, the fathers of the two born Muslims in Tsakani allegedly became Muslim as a result of sickness *(ukongo)* before migrating to Kaloleni. My intention is to show that this is a ritual and cosmological adaptation to the specialized roles newly undertaken by these young entrepreneurs and is a way of marking them off from poorer elders.

New Ritual Categories

Emerging entrepreneurs constitute one of four categories of persons who appear prone to possession by Islamic spirits. A second category includes a very few women who subsequently migrate to Mombasa or Malindi, where they manage to raise the cash, perhaps from prostitution, to repay the bridewealth given over for them and so free themselves from their marriages. A third category includes a few female and young male diviners. A fourth includes a small number of Duruma settlers in Kaloleni, whose settlement and land rights have been questioned in recent years. I need no longer deal specifically with the latter.

The significant thing about all these categories is that they are either marginal in certain social respects, like the female or young male diviners, or they appear to contravene particular customary expectations, as do the young entrepreneurs who amass wealth, thus reversing the value that economic control should be wielded exclusively by elders, or the few women who foil the system of male control.[4]

Though it is no more than a tendency, we have here an example of innovating or, from the elders' viewpoint, deviant minority sections of the community's legitimizing their activities by partial conversion to a religion which contrasts in its practices with the traditional one followed by the vast majority of Giriama. It may seem odd to talk of partial conversion. The point is that these innovators do not totally abandon their participation in activities based on Giriama religious and cosmological ideas. They continue to make use of Giriama doctors and diviners, to attend and contribute to the cost of the funerals of relatives and neighbours, to suspect others of sorcery, and even to tend the *koma* (ancestral pegs) in their homesteads during a crisis. They have selected from Islam only its prohibition on commensality and the duty to fast. None of the Swahili Muslims in Kaloleni accepts these innovators as "pure" *(safi)* Muslims. For them, prayer and attendance at the Kaloleni Friday mosque are additional requisite qualities of Muslim status. Yet, they accept that these innovators have genuinely been possessed by true Islamic spirits which have demanded their abstention from Giriama food and drink. They concede so much and no more, which is all that the innovators require.

In accepting only one set of Islamic ritual rules—namely, that discouraging Muslim and non-Muslim Giriama from eating and drinking together—the entrepreneurs establish a partial social barrier between themselves and many of their kin and neighbours. This creates ambiguity in the relationship: the entrepreneurs need their fellow Giriama as witnesses, informers, and potential sellers; but they have to avoid allowing this dependence to become too one-sided, lest it cause a drain on their limited resources by constant demands for small loans which bring little or no return.

If it becomes difficult for ritual reasons to eat and drink with a man in a society in which commensality is an idiom through which relations of intimacy and alliance are expressed, then it may become correspondingly easy to stave off repeated requests for financial help from a number of such men. Giriama put the matter in a different but familiar idiom: they say that this withdrawal from commensal relations lessens the chances of a wealthier man's being poisoned or ensorcelled (both referred to as *utsai*) by jealous neighbours and relatives. As I have explained, the drinking together of palm wine, in particular, has great symbolic value for Giriama and connotes sharing. Normally it is impossible to refuse an invitation to drink without causing offence. But Muslims are excused on legitimate ritual grounds.

However, this ritual device for deterring the creation of intensely obligatory personal relations must be used selectively and carefully. Some men who are more useful as witnesses or informers than others constitute a better investment and so can be indulged more than others. They can be given some help toward the bridewealth of a son or toward the expenses of a funeral or the medical charges incurred by a member of their family. Or they can be given places of honour at a funerary or other ceremonial feast lavishly sponsored by the entrepreneur. At these feasts some or all of the beasts assembled are slaughtered by a Muslim for the benefit of Muslims present. Though they partake of different meat, both Muslims and non-Muslims are thereby able to eat together on the same public occasion, something which, for practical reasons is unlikely to occur in private homes.

Muslim Giriama entrepreneurs, both therapeutic and born, are thus able to use their distinct ritual status to create an ambivalence in their relations with other Giriama. They are clearly insiders in so far as they accept the mediatory role of Giriama elders and much of the customary law on which the elders' power is based. But they are outsiders in so far as they can withdraw from close personal ties of the kind which are likely to lead to an encumbrance of economically unprofitable relations.

Born Giriama Muslims fall much more at the outsider end of the continuum than do therapeutic Muslims. They claim that many of their customs are like those of the Swahili Muslims. Because this outsider aspect of their status was ascribed to them at birth, they are not in a position of having to explain a switch in religious affiliation. But the therapeutic Muslims *are*. Their partial conversion is explained as having been necessary on pain of death: the dictates of the Islamic spirits had to be obeyed in order to loosen the grip of an otherwise fatal illness.

Who legitimizes this extremely useful ambivalent status, which benefits enterprising men and—though I have done no more than mention them—women, who reject the traditional roles ascribed to them? One would not expect it to be the elders, who as gerontocrats are hardly likely to sanction the award of special privileges to those whom they are supposed to control. Indeed, some of the elders are neighbourhood doctors, who themselves need someone to validate their claims to skill in Islamic medicines. Quite unconnectedly, the Swahili Muslims of Kaloleni provide one source of legitimacy, and Giriama diviners provide another.

The Swahili of Kaloleni are of the Jomvu or Al Jaufiy sub-group. They regard their true home as Mombasa, from which they procure the fish and few vegetables which they sell in Kaloleni trading centre, where they have also built a small village of ten families. The stalls they use for their trading are owned by a Giriama and are on his land. This typifies their status as small-time traders who work and live in Kaloleni on sufferance because they sell a useful relish, but who have never been economically dominant. They have the only Friday mosque in Kaloleni and have their own resident leader *(mwalimu)*. This man and a few other Jomvu willingly discuss points of alleged Islamic theology with anyone who is interested. The religious leader frequently urges men to become Muslims, but with little success. But neighbourhood doctors and therapeutic Muslims do associate with him: they invite him to their homes and particularly to funerary sacrifices, where he or another Muslim will slaughter a selection of beasts. By talking and associating with the leader and other Swahili in Kaloleni, doctors and therapeutic Muslims publicise the validity of their claims to have access to Islamic medicines or to have been involuntarily possessed by Islamic spirits. The Swahili thus have the status of neutral referees, so to speak, in a competition between doctors who are prominent elders and those who threaten to undermine their influence—the emerging young entrepreneurs.

The belief that therapeutic Muslims are involuntarily possessed and so have no alternative to obeying the dictates of Islamic spirits is, of course, particularly convenient in a society in which conversion to Islam has always been regarded as a mild act of betrayal. Enterprising farmers would surely be hindered by the accusations of betrayal that might follow a sudden intentional switch to Muslim status. Thus branded, how would they recruit their witnesses, informers, and sellers of property? It is the Swahili who validate their claims to involuntary possession after their conversion, but it is Giriama diviners who actually diagnose this form of possession.

Diviners who make such diagnoses may themselves have been possessed by an Islamic spirit. Almost certainly, they will have been possessed by Giriama spirits. As with the neighbourhood doctors, the wider their range of skills, the better for their profession. As far as it is possible to assess, diviners, too, appear to have increased in numbers as more cash has been made available in the society. This said, the diviners stand otherwise in complete contrast to the doctors.

First, doctors are always senior men, while diviners are nowadays either women or young men (always married, to my knowledge). A few of the doctors used to divine when they were younger. There is no apparent preference for men over women diviners, and in neighbourhoods known to me around Tsakani there seemed to be only slightly more women than men. Many more women than men are possessed—I estimated a ratio of about 200 women to every man. However, many of these women are possessed at the dances ostensibly held to placate spirits at least once a week in and around Tsakani. This is called possession by spirits of the body *(pepo za mwirini)* and is distinct from the much less frequent possession by spirits of the head or mind *(pepo za kitswa)*, of which Islamic spirits are a type. This type of possession awards powers of divination to the possessed person, who thus acquires power of mediumship. Unlike the doctors, therefore, diviners do not merely purchase the tools of their trade in order to establish their practice.[5]

A second main difference between doctors and diviners is that, while doctors charge according to reputation, with a minimum charge of two shillings for a session, diviners can never charge more than 50 cents (half a shilling) for a session or for a séance, which may be longer and more elaborate in its dramatic expression.

A third main difference is that diviners only diagnose the cause of an illness or misfortune, or else give advice on how to buy luck. They do not effect cures or satisfy vengeance by supplying sorcery. They provide only the preliminary diagnosis. For the real treatment, they recommend a neighbourhood doctor or sometimes, depending on the patient's circumstances, a more prominent doctor in Mombasa or Malindi. Neighbourhood doctors thus treat diviners with respect despite their obvious juniority in the Giriama system of medical practice. Since the diviners are also, with the Swahili, an authority by which therapeutic Islam is diagnosed, they too can be regarded as neutral

A Tsakani diviner displays some of the tools of his trade.

bystanders who referee the opposition between elders and enterprising young farmers or any others who would defy the gerontocracy.

Therapeutic Islam thus benefits people such as the young enterprising farmers by enabling them to legitimize social deviance or marginality—that is to say, innovation. This being so, we must wonder whether enterprising farmers or dissatisfied women deliberately feign possession in order to acquire this legitimation. We are left with little more than the anthropologist's own impression of whether or not this is so. Giriama certainly point to specific instances of false possession. But, whatever psychological factors may induce them, it would seem from my observation that genuine trances do occur and are not consciously simulated. Perhaps trances are induced by pre-conscious acceptance of a belief system. There seems, anyway, to be no reason to doubt that those involved in the system either as observers, practitioners, or possessed, believe in it.

The fact that specific categories of people seem more prone to possession than others is an example of religious beliefs and activities' coming to fit the needs of a changing society. Abner Cohen describes how the Islamic Tijaniyya Order fitted the need of a Hausa trading community in Ibadan to organize itself more corporately in the face of a challenge to its existence. In Kaloleni an ecological factor, the extending palm belt, has facilitated economic specialisation in the past twenty-five years and has created the development of wealth differences and a re-definition of roles of influence. In this process of re-definition, some categories have been discovering new places in society: young enterprising farmers, elders and neighbourhood doctors, diviners, and women who question their customary roles. For the Giriama, Islam is peripheral, in that only a few of its ritual rules are accepted. These are added to the indigenous body of beliefs and customs which remain central to Giriama social organisation (cf. Lewis 1966).

Conclusion

I have described how the people of Tsakani have responded to the polarization of economic and ritual roles which, seen from another perspective, is a polarization of family heads, who are socially designated as young and old. The next stage of analysis is to illustrate the circumstances which have given rise to the present distribution of power and influence.

These are circumstances which have been documented in other societies and derive from a contradiction of two types of expenditure. One has been called contingent expenditure and is necessitated by customary obligations, sometimes of a ceremonial nature, including bridewealth, funeral expenses, traditional medical costs, sacrifice, and the maintenance of ritual status. A second type of expenditure is directed toward personal economic expansion, as in the purchase of land and other property, and results in greater economic control of the community by a specific group or category. It is possible to regard the first type of expenditure as an attempt at investment in maintaining the *existing* system of authority relations. That is to say, it is a form of expenditure which is restricted to customary spheres of exchange which reaffirm a network of statuses. Thus, Bailey (1957, pp. 62–73) shows how in a village in Orissa, India, the warrior caste group continues to meet customary demands for expenditure on funerals and weddings without due regard to the changing economic circumstances which enable what formerly was a lower caste, the distillers, to compete with them for economic and political power. L. Caplan (1970, p. 91) describes the process by which a Nepalese tribespeople, called the Limbu, continues to meet similar customary obligations among themselves, even at the cost of indebting themselves to Hindu immigrants. And, on the same continent, Elwin (1955, pp. 445–459) describes how Saora individuals become indebted to a neighbouring people called the Christian Doms.

Among the Giriama of Kaloleni there is a similar process at work which is, however, internal to them and does not work to the benefit of a neighbouring ethnic group. As explained, the position of older homestead heads as judicial mediators, witnesses, and ritual spokesmen, depends on continued recognition of the value of agnation as an organizing principle for allocating property and arranging marriages.

The exchange of bridewealth for women and their offspring among Giriama is the primary means by which sub-clans and clans are distinguished and the general principle of agnation upheld. The inheritance of widows and property, which is supervised by clan elders, is an aspect of this sphere of exchange. In order to maintain the *status quo,* therefore, the elders have to invest in this sphere: bride-wealth, in exchange for the reproductive powers in a woman, must continue to be the only means by which agnatic families can be augmented. This must be so, regardless of the rise in the absolute value of bridewealth payments among Giriama and despite the fact that cash exclusively is now used as a mode of payment in Kaloleni.

If elders could exercise a monopoly over the two commodities in this exchange system—money and women—then their authority would be undisturbed. They may indeed succeed in controlling or restricting the status of women. But they cannot retain a monopoly over the use of cash because a minority of younger, enterprising farmers are investing in palms and land and thus are challenging the *status quo.*

In the next chapter I describe this new investment in land and palms and show how it has altered the idiom of exchange relations from one phrased in terms of agnation and affinity to one expressed more as individual contract.

NOTES

1. When I left the field in 1967, copra prices had continued to decline, while cashew-nut prices were steadily rising. Cashew-nut trees are clearly a better investment, but are still far fewer than coconut palms, and it remains to be seen how far they will supplant the palms.

2. The Kaloleni Christian Missionary Society hospital regularly sends newly discovered Giriama herbs which are used as medicines to a research unit at Mulago Hospital, Kampala, Uganda, and was able to give me this and other related information.

3. Compare J. Goody (1957), who speculates that among Ashanti increased wealth and use of cash

instead of kind expanded the professional opportunities in medicine and divination.

4. Christianity provides a similar means of escape from certain customary expectations, usually at a higher rung of the entrepreneurial ladder (see the case of the wealthy businessman in Chapter 8). I have not the space here to deal with its different implications. There is one practising Christian among the thirty economic managers in Tsakani.

5. Divinatory powers are said frequently to be inherited from a deceased relative of the same sex of a previous generation. Some informants also claimed that female diviners could only trace such powers matrilineally. (See also P. Caplan 1969.)

5. Custom Threatened: The Capitalist Spirit

Settlement and the Switch to Copra

By about the beginning of the twentieth century, Pax Britannica had succeeded in preventing military encounters between the Giriama and other nearby ethnic groups such as the Kwavi Masai, Kamba, and Galla. But the Giriama had continued to use their skills of rapid mobility within their extensive hinterland bush and were thus able to elude British demands for tax and labour. Their determined resistance to meet these demands led to the Giriama Rising of 1914.

The Giriama were defeated. They had earned for themselves a chapter in history for organising one of the first anti-colonial rebellions in East Africa, but the spark of armed resistance was never seen among them again during the colonial era. Nor did they continue to make rapid and extensive movements within Giriama country.

Indeed, it is at that point that many Giriama appear to have accepted a more settled way of life. A few became voluntary labour migrants in towns or on plantations. Some moved from the bush to Kaloleni location, to areas like Tsakani, where, on the evidence of family histories, there were only three or four homesteads in the early twenties. The newcomers extended the fringe of coconut palms in their direction, so that they were eventually enveloped by it. In those early days they saw the palms only as a source of wine and supplementary food.

In the twenties and early thirties there were few cash-earning labour migrants in Kaloleni, and copra had not become the important cash crop that it was among the Rabai, ten miles to the south. Money did not therefore quickly supplant livestock as a medium of exchange for land or as bridewealth, though bridewealth might sometimes consist of a combination of cash and livestock.[1]

World War II may be taken as the period dividing two eras: the first dating from the Rising, when the copra-based economic value of palms was being more widely realised, but when most immovable property transacted was still land and not yet palms, with livestock being the principal medium of exchange; and the second the post-war era, when there apparently was a switch in the Kaloleni area from livestock to cash for land and tree transactions and when a steadily increasing number of transactions involved palms, alone or together with the land on which they stood. For the purpose of measuring changes in the quantity and manner in which land and palms were transacted, it seems reasonable to adopt the Giriama view that 1944 was the "real" year dividing the two eras. Giriama do not refer to this year but to the time when the rains failed and brought on the famine of wheat *(ndzala ya ngano)*. This is the most frequently cited chronological event of contemporary times. Births, marriages, and deaths are dated by reference to it. An investigation of marital histories suggests that since then the inflationary tendencies in Giriama bridewealth have been greatly accelerated and that increasingly more cash than livestock has been used. More precisely, we know that 1945 saw the return home of the few Giriama who had served with the army in World War II. The money they brought back was never much, even by local standards, and was greatly eclipsed by the amount that the Asian traders injected into the local economy through the purchase of copra and other produce. But it played its part in the greater monetization of the spheres of exchange involving bridewealth, land, and palms.

The internal palm-wine trade was the link between the two eras. It only produced wealth for a few men, but, more important, it stimulated a desire for more palms in accordance with the rising population and the extension of the trade. In the middle and late thirties Asian traders moved to Kaloleni and bought copra in progressively greater quantities, so that by the end of the war this commodity was replacing palm wine as the principle money-earner.

This change-over was accelerated after 1952, when, as many Giriama in the area recall, the price of copra suddenly soared from the 1950 price of 9.70 shillings to 25 shillings for a *frasila* (36 pounds) and stayed high for several years. By 1967 it had dropped to 16 shillings. Indeed, there was clear evidence in 1967 of renewed interest in palm wine as a useful second-string cash crop, but copra remained the prime crop and, together with the sale of whole coconuts, continued to stimulate individual acquisitions of palms.

The switch to copra is related to four other factors. First, the amount of palm wine that can be sold among fellow Giriama is limited, whereas the international demand for copra in the mid-fifties seemed unlimited. Second, the technical problems of the palm-wine trade, described earlier, require the producer to depend on a long chain of employees, or helpers, so that, though turnovers may be high, profits are relatively low. By contrast, the Asians, and after them the government-sponsored farmers' co-operative relieved the copra and coconut producer of the problems of sale, distribution, and delivery. Third, in 1947 the government relaxed the requirements for obtaining trading licences. Before, virtually only Asians and Arabs had been able to afford the initial capital required. After 1947 a few Giriama started very small businesses. With the help of loans from Asians for whom they had previously worked and with whom, in some cases, they continued to work, some developed their enterprises substantially. As well as setting up shops and buying buses or lorries, they bought large holdings of palms and so established a pattern throughout Kaloleni to be imitated by ordinary, but enterprising farmers.

Fourth, with the approach of Kenya's independence, the government decided that the private middleman in the copra trade should be eliminated, in order to increase the profits to producers. In 1964 the Kaloleni Farmers' Co-operative Society was established, with the exclusive right to trade in copra, coconuts, and certain other commodities. The government encouraged ordinary farmers to invest in growing more palms. For Asians, the withdrawal of their licences to trade in copra, coconuts, and the other produce now dealt with by the co-operative represented the loss of a major source of profit. For the smaller number of Giriama middlemen the loss was not so great, since they could expand their position as producers by continuing to amass holdings of palms and land. The Asians have never been legally entitled to do this.

From that time Giriama entrepreneurs could no longer obtain substantial loans from Asians. But they could turn, instead, to two new sources which became available with independence. One was the government agricultural department (formally, the Ministry of Agriculture), and the other the Kilifi county council, which would provide loans for business and farming equipment or premises, though officially not, as the Asians did, for the purchase of palms and land. These loans are given to men of proven ability who already have large palm holdings and who use the loans to diversify their enterprises.

The Asians were equally vigilant about their debtors. They were not legally able to take land and palms as security for their loans and therefore only made large loans to those Giriama whom they knew to be economically astute. These were men who had acted as brokers in persuading fellow Giriama farmers to sell copra and other produce to their specific Asian patrons. Similarly, the government agricultural department and the county council require some evidence of the worthiness of an applicant for a loan. This is the baseline status needed by any applicant. It is only thereafter that favouritism and the conditions which lead to it may determine whether the application is successful.

Loans are thus one source of capital open to the established businessman or farmer. What about the men on whom I am focusing, who are not regarded as having reached this rung of the ladder? How do they raise the money to acquire palms and land?

Raising Capital

Most of the enterprising farmers began their careers in the boom period of the fifties by making their first purchase of palms and/or land partly or wholly with money saved from wage-earnings. They are typically eldest sons who have had to relinquish wage-employment on the death of a father, to assume headship of his homestead. A wage-income thus ceases to accumulate as further capital. Moreover, the current surplus demand for wage-employment throughout Kenya and the generally higher standard of education required has now made that a less likely source of initial capital for most Giriama in Kaloleni. As explained, few sons who are earning are prepared to risk investing money by buying palms or land through their fathers, for fear that at their deaths the property be swallowed in the common patrimony. Enterprising farmers may not, therefore, always expect help from sons in wage-employment. They turn to two other sources of continuing capital accumulation, which they may more easily control: the cash proceeds of a harvest of copra or other produce and the cash bridewealth received for a sister or daughter.

The cash earned from the sale of copra or coconuts should first be spent on subsistence needs in the homestead, if the palms are held in trust for a number of agnates and not owned by just one man. But, if a man has sole rights of ownership over some of the palms, the income from those palms is regarded as his to do with as he pleases, as is true of wage-earnings.

Similarly, the cash bridewealth received for a dependent sister or daughter, classificatory or otherwise, may sometimes be used as capital for the purchase of palms. This is more easily possible if daughters outnumber sons, who are not thereby deprived of their own bridewealth when they marry. It is also possible if sons or male wards are too young to need the bridewealth immediately: the father or trustee may then invest the cash in buying palms in the expectation of recouping sufficient capital in the years ahead to provide bridewealth for his male dependents.

In other words, apart from loans, capital for the purchase of palms is raised by tapping three main sources of cash. Initially, wage-earnings have been used. Thereafter, use is made of cash from the sale of crops and of bridewealth received upon the marriage of female dependents. Still the most common place for keeping cash seems to be a man's own homestead, even for sums of one or two thousand shillings. Three men in Tsakani have bank or post-office accounts, while others deposit sums for safekeeping with carefully chosen Giriama and Asian shopkeepers. Whether or not a man can use these savings to buy palms, as opportunities arise, obviously depends on his expenses, which, in the last analysis, depend on his personal skills and on luck.

He needs to be skillful as a farmer in order to meet his family's subsistence demands from his own land without having to buy food from the shops or from other farmers. Skilled farmers so time the planting of maize and cassava in different fields that, even in the event of late or heavy and prolonged rains, they will have most of the food they need. Admittedly, apart from one or two who are able to store sufficient grain from a previous season, none can combat the disaster following total drought. But there is clearly some scope for initiative in planning for subsistence needs through farming techniques and so avoiding a drain on savings.

Misfortune plays an important part, too. Sickness requires cure, and prolonged medical treatment can be expensive. Funerals require lavish expenditure, but no one can plan for an above-average number of deaths in his family within a short period. A man may be blessed with many sons for whom he must find bride-wealth, but few daughters to offset this loss. To the benefit of another, the converse may be the case. It is small wonder that the neighbourhood doctors and diviners continue to cater to all men and have increased in numbers as luck and misfortune are sought or avoided.

From personal observation, however, it is clear that in a large enough sample skills can be seen to win out over luck in the emergence of successful farmers. The skills are not just those of good farming. They are also those of the good economic manager, who is simply the man who budgets so well that his gains exceed his losses and give him sufficient capital to buy palms as soon as he hears that they are for sale. The network of informers and contacts that quickly enables him to make the "hot" purchase is another result of his skills and is of particular interest in a sociological analysis.

Let me now illustrate the effects in Tsakani of the switch to copra as the principal money-earner. I shall do this by dividing the period from 1944, the year of the famine of the wheat, to 1967 into two twelve-year periods and contrasting the number and types of transaction involving land and palms in Tsakani. This gives 1944 to 1955, inclusive, as the first period and 1956 to 1967 as the second. It is convenient to have 1955 and 1956 as the bridging years, since it was by then that the soaring copra price of 1952 had surely had its effect on most men in Tsakani, causing them to realise the new value of palms. Even those who had not yet bought palms could not help being affected by the "palm fever".

Wealth Differences

The number of transactions of palms and land undertaken by Tsakani family heads was eighteen in the first twelve years. But this more than doubled to forty-seven during the second period. Population increase alone does not account for this rise, which has to be seen as the result of a definite scramble for palms by individuals.

This 100 percent sample of Tsakani land and palm transactions from 1944 to 1967 is obviously small. But in nearly all respects it does bear out people's views on changes in the nature of the transactions and of relations among the people who have been party to them.

I need here to distinguish what I shall call limited mortgage, unlimited mortgage, and outright purchase. Outright purchase is clearly the permanent alienation of usually (nowadays) both palms and the land on which they stand. Unlimited mortgage refers to pledged land and/or palms which may be redeemed technically at any time on repayment of the original loan made by the mortgagee. Limited mortgage refers to pledged land and/or palms which *must* be redeemed by the mortgagor within an agreed number of years. If the mortgagee (the creditor) has not been repaid by the end of the agreed period, then he acquires permanent total rights in the property. It should be noted here that, unlike some indigenous mortgage systems in other parts of the world (see L. Caplan 1970, p. 91, and P. Lloyd 1962, p. 310), the loan must be repaid in full, regardless of how much money the mortgagee may have made from using the palms and land over the years.

Giriama themselves distinguish between purchase and mortgage, and between limited and unlimited mortgage. Giriama say that only in recent years have limited mortgages been introduced into Tsakani. And, sure enough, in the period from 1956 to 1967, eleven (about 23 percent) of the transactions were limited mortgages, whereas none were during the preceding twelve years (see Table 5). Correspondingly, the number of unlimited mortgages has decreased approxi-

TABLE 5. TYPES OF TRANSACTIONS OF PALMS AND LAND IN TSAKANI*

	unlimited mortgage	limited mortgage	outright purchase	number of transactions
1944–1955	33.3%	none	66.7%	18
1956–1967	4.3%	23.4%	72.3%	47

*Of all transactions in the two consecutive periods, 43 percent were of palms alone, 35 percent of palms and land combined, and only 21 percent of land alone.

mately from 33 percent to 4 percent from the first to the second period. The proportion of outright purchases has remained virtually the same, increasing only slightly from about 66 percent to about 72 percent, though larger individual plots have been transferred in this way in the second period.

The local Giriama explanation for the substitution of unlimited mortgage by limited mortgage suggests awareness of the development of a more contractual idiom of exchange. They say that nowadays men take land and palms in exchange for cash not simply to help a friend, neighbour, or relative out of trouble, but to expand their own holdings. Few persons ever redeem unlimited mortgages, let alone limited ones, so that stipulating a limited mortgage as a condition of contract gives the cash donor early inalienable rights to plant more palms on the property as he pleases. The big advantage to the mortgagee is that the loan he extends for a limited mortgage is less than he would pay in outright purchase of property. He thus gambles on the reasonable likelihood that the mortgagor will fail to redeem in time and so stands to profit from a cheap buy. Only two of the eleven limited mortgages during the second period were redeemed.

A second reason for the replacement of unlimited by limited mortgage is the recently introduced court ruling that a mortgagee cannot plant palms on land which has been pledged to him. Since many enterprising farmers view land as having its greatest value only when it carries palms, this ruling clearly frustrates their expansionist aims for land that is pledged to them indefinitely. There is therefore an increasing tendency among them to take land, as well as palms, in limited mortgage.

In practice, therefore, the pledging of land and palms in limited mortgage is likely to result in their permanent alienation from the vendor. The increasing use of limited mortgage, together with an almost unchanged but already high rate of outright purchase, has meant that proportionally much more property was permanently alienated during the second than the first period.

A second difference in scale has been in the general increase in the size of holdings transacted during the second period. It is unnecessary to reproduce the details, but the average amounts of land and palms transacted have actually increased. Since accumulators are less numerous than losers of property in Tsakani, we can speak here of a process by which a minority of farmers has increasingly gained absolute and permanent rights in a larger proportion of the most important economic assets. Wealth is being concentrated in fewer hands.

The Losers and the Accumulators

Here I must pause to define some terms. The three men frequently referred to in Chapter 4 clearly deserve the title of entrepreneur by any common-sense definition. They are also enterprising farmers, in that they became established through the accumulation of many palms, which they then used as capital and which they are continuing to accumulate. But there are other enterprising farmers in Tsakani who are accumulating palms, but who have not yet branched out into any form of business (e.g. a shop, a hotel, or a transport service). They occupy the lower rungs of the entrepreneurial ladder. They are on the way up but have not yet arrived.

In Tsakani I will reserve the term *entrepreneur* for the three men already described, to whom it most aptly applies. I will reserve the general term *accumulators* for other enterprising farmers who do not run businesses but who have expanded their holdings of palms and land. Their expansionist aims are publicly recognised, are the subject of gossip, discussion, recrimination, and admiration, and therefore are "social facts". I shall call those who have not expanded or who have progressively lost palms and land through sale, mortgage, or unsuccessfully defended claims the *losers*. They, too, are marked out as men who have, for "good" reasons as well as "foul", undergone economic deprivation or, in a few cases, have simply failed to take advantage of the opportunities for capital accumulation offered by palms in the post-war scramble. Again, gossip, scandal, and sober discussion are the media by which their deprivation or failure is known and evaluated.

The distinction between the accumulators and the losers is here subjective, in that it is measured among Giriama by such an objectively unreliable yardstick as gossip. But it has been possible within the small and intimately known sample of thirty economic managers in Tsakani actually to record who has accumulated or lost palms during the economic changes of the past twenty-five years. Few of the accumulators are other than self-made men. That is to say, they do not appear to have been unduly helped by handsome legacies (factors of this kind will surely be more relevant in the forthcoming generation). Finally, the accumulators are almost all wealthier men, whose assets are among the largest, as depicted in Table 4. It is fair to claim that men's actual assets, gains, and losses do parallel closely their reputations as economic managers.

In Tsakani the accumulators number ten and the losers, twenty. An important distinguishing feature is that all ten accumulators have at least some open land which is ploughed by one or other of two tractors recently made available for hire in Kaloleni: one of them is actually owned by one of the Tsakani entrepreneurs and the other, by the Kaloleni Farmers' Co-operative Society. The cost of ploughing and harrowing is 60 shillings per acre. By contrast, few of the losers have sufficient land to warrant the use of a plough, and only three do so. However, both accumulators and losers continue to rely on their women for hoe-cultivation of the occasional small patches between clusters of palms, many of which cannot be reached by tractor. Most of the accumulators employ Duruma migrants on a casual basis during digging, planting, and harvesting, though it is only the three entrepreneurs who do so on a regular contractual basis. Losers tend not to employ farm workers, though they may help and be helped by relatives in times of need, as when a wife, daughter, daughter-in-law, or son is unable to work the farm because of sickness.

It should be re-emphasised here that Tsakani, in which the managers live, is not defined according to such economic criteria as the flow of property transactions or the distribution of property within the area. Property holdings may be highly fragmented, so that a manager in Tsakani may own palms and land in areas other than that in which he lives. Similarly, there are palms and some land in Tsakani owned by persons living some distance from it. Tsakani is a neighbourhood defined by the proximity to each other of specified homesteads. The managers whom I dub accumulators acquire property from areas throughout Kaloleni, while those of the losers who sell do so to persons outside, as well as within, Tsakani.

Nevertheless, the ten accumulators and the twenty losers, in addition to being neighbours, are all members of the same economic and social system. Only a few of the accumulators in Tsakani may actually have bought from locally resident losers. But this does not lessen the apparent distance between them of ideological difference and moral interpretation. Tsakani has boundaries, mainly imposed by myself as an observer. In reality, the accumulators represent in the eyes of the losers the characteristics of accumulators throughout Kaloleni.

From figures obtained from the Kaloleni co-operative I estimate that no more than 100 of the location's 450 homestead heads within the palm belt are accumulators, according to these criteria. Tsakani does seem, therefore, to have proportionally rather more than the usual number of accumulators.

Of the ten accumulators in Tsakani, seven have fixed assets in the form of palms valued at more than 3,000 shillings, one at more than 2,000 shillings, and one at more than 1,000 shillings. Only one has assets of less than 1,000 shillings. Of the twenty losers, thirteen have assets of less than 1,000 shillings, three less than 2,000 shillings, and one less than 3,000 shillings, while only three continue to have assets worth more than 3,000 shillings, due in each case to large inheritances and not to personal acquisition of a contractual nature.

The accumulators tend, therefore, to include post-war *nouveaux riches,* while the losers tend to include economic laggards or victims of the changes since the war. Included among the ten accumulators are the three young entrepreneurs whom I distinguished as having fixed assets worth more than 7,000 shillings. By contrast, the four traditional doctors mentioned, who are in their fifties and sixties, are among the twenty losers, two of them having assets of less than 1,000 shillings, and two having less than 2,000 shillings and 3,000 shillings, respectively. The economic, ritual, and generational polarities discussed above are thus nicely summarised in their contrasting financial statuses.

This is, then, a situation of increasing economic specialisation. It began slowly when the Asians in Kaloleni first bought up copra in significant quantities in the 1930s but was undoubtedly accelerated in the years after World War II, especially from the mid-fifties until the present time, following the rapid rise in the price of copra. This specialisation of economic roles has the effect of defining more clearly roles of a manifestly non-economic nature. The relatively recent occurrence of this phenomenon among a small, easily observable neighbourhood grouping enables us to analyse the changes in interpersonal relations which have resulted from this process.

The Demands of Kinship and Affinity

We know that in many such situations of rapid economic specialisation, older, more conservative folk decry the individualism which contemporary life and a cash economy are said to bring. A constant theme of conversation among older men in Kaloleni is the reminder to themselves and others that the very few prosperous individualists are, nevertheless, "still their children", who rely on them for advice on ritual, customary procedure, and sometimes adjudication. "They are destroying our customs" is the somewhat resigned accusation made against them. Yet, the accusers will in other contexts admit the necessity of conventional forms of "modern progress".

If we focus on land and palm transactions, we see that the most obvious stated conflict between allegedly old and new values is in the spheres of kinship and affinity. What this really means is that the idiom of contractual relationships has changed.

The gerontocrats' ideal is that, if land and immovable property have to be sold, then at least they should be sold among kin, and even affines, if necessary. But the new tendency is seen as flouting the ideal and conforming with the emphasis on greater commercialism and individualism: landed property is being sold or mortgaged to people who either have no relationship of kinship or affinity with the holder or for whom such relationships are irrelevant.

In one sense the figures we have support the Giriama assertion that there has been a shift in contractual idiom and ideal. There is absolutely no difference between the two post-war periods in the proportion of transactions involving those who designate each other in some way as kin or affines. The proportion for each period is 28 percent. What is significant, however, is that the transactions between kin and affines in the second period involved considerably less property than those between non-kin and non-affines. Taken together with Giriama pronouncements on the matter, this does seem to support the notion that the larger,

"more commercial" sales and mortgages are being increasingly forged by preference among non-kin and that the idiom of kinship and affinity is required less as
a sanction for contracts, which is resulting in permanent alienation of land.

I would ask two related questions. First, which kin and affines occur in these
transactions? Second, why are transactions between kin and affines retained, even
though they involve proportionally little property?

Taking the two periods as a whole, there is a slight difference in proportions
of kin and affines who have been parties to transactions. Eleven transactions are
between kin and seven between affines. More significant is the fact that ten of the
eleven kin transactions are actually between agnates. This certainly complies with
Giriama notions regarding economic relations among kin. The two important
categories, they say, are agnates (people of your *mbari*) and affines (people linked
to you through the marriage of a member of your family and, by extension, your
mbari). Of the eighteen kin and affinal transactions, only one is between a mother's brother and sister's son, and even this is a classificatory terminological
relationship which was only invoked for purposes of the contract.

From the point of view of Tsakani residents requiring property, and allowing
for transactions within Tsakani, the range of agnatic relationships in these transactions is: real grandfather (two transactions); brother of real grandfather (two
transactions); grandfather's patrilateral parallel cousin, father's full brother, father's patrilateral parallel cousin, own patrilateral parallel cousin (one transaction, each); and unspecified agnates of the same generation (two transactions).

The range of affinal relationships is: son-in-law's father (two transactions);
wife's brother, son-in-law's brother, wife's matrilateral parallel cousin, wife's
matrilateral cross-cousin, and classificatory son's son-in-law (one transaction
each).

One can hardly sub-classify the sample of transactions further. But one important point remains. This is that seven of the ten transactions between agnates
involved palms only, a fact in obvious support of the Giriama statement that land
"already belongs to the *mbari* lineage or clan and cannot therefore be sold to a
member of it, though the palms have been planted by an individual in the *mbari*
and are exclusively his to dispose of as he pleases". In other words, transactions
between agnates are most likely to involve the transmission of palms, alone. This
means that the enterprising farmer cannot pull down old palms and plant new
ones in such a transaction and so explains why he prefers to acquire property from
non-agnates. Whether or not he acquires property from an affine, or, to put it
another way, whether he is prepared to express the relationship in terms of
affinity, depends very much on the nature of the relationship before the transaction takes place.

The wide range in both agnatic and affinal relationships in even the small
sub-samples presented here suggest for each a wide net of options. The flexibility
both of the term and of the concept *mbari* reflects the possibility of articulating
genealogically very distant as well as close agnates in striking bargains. The range
of possible affinal relationships is, among Giriama, almost infinitesimal, through

the system of serial linking by which two families can express a relationship through even a score of intermediary families.

There are two disadvantages in acquiring palms and land from agnates and affines. One is that they involve small amounts of palms and land, often isolated from much of the accumulator's other property. The second is that they tend to represent no more than a marginally good investment to the accumulator, who may have agreed to take the property in response to a plea for cash and have paid a little above the market price. The idiom of kinship and affinity blunts the negotiable edge in contractual relations.

Why, then, should the accumulator bother to enter into such agreements, in view of the obvious greater advantage of acquiring property on an open market unencumbered by the tiresome restrictions and obligations that accompany kinship and affinity? The Giriama explanation is the usual one, to the effect that "a man cannot refuse to help a kinsman or affine who approaches him for a loan". It is certainly true that moral pressures and sanctions of disapproval can be powerful weapons of persuasion. But we can look beyond the Giriama view and suggest a further explanation. Since agnation and, by implication, affinity underly the local gerontocracy—that is, the status of witnesses—and since the support of witnesses has to be retained by rival accumulators, we can see these transactions as part of a whole range of concessions which any successful accumulator must make to men of influence.

At an individual level, witnesses may gratefully accept this recognition of their influence, although as a category they figure among the economic losers. Yet, as individuals they continue at different times to sell or mortgage their property. They are involved in an irreconcilable situation. On the one hand, they owe their influence to continued acknowledgement of their expertise in customary law and ritual. On the other hand, because of that position, they are compelled by customary forms of contingent expenditure to dispose of their economic assets.

Contingent Demands

The most common of these financial needs are: (a) the cash bridewealth for a son, a brother or ward, or oneself; (b) expenses for a funeral or sacrifice; (c) the costs of having a traditional doctor during a long illness of a family member; and (d) money for food after a poor harvest or for other similar contingencies.

Bridewealth and funerary expenditure has risen greatly since 1944. A father or guardian is responsible for the total bridewealth of a son or ward. This is now paid wholly in cash. Few sons are in wage-labour, but those who are do not contribute to the bridewealth, as is now the custom in many other parts of Kenya. Giriama funerals are supposed to be sponsored by the closest agnate of the deceased or, in the case of a deceased married woman, by her husband. More than being simply obligatory, the funerals must be lavish occasions, the magnificence of which match, and frequently exceed, the resources of the nominal sponsors.

Natural or man-made misfortunes, of which the greatest is sickness, strike into the lives of men and their families with a suddenness which defies resistance or delay. Cures must be sought, sometimes at great expense, from a range of traditional doctors, whose various techniques are applied until success, or death, ensues. A poor harvest—a frequent occurrence after a drought or untimely heavy rains—causes people to turn to the shops or their more enterprising neighbours for purchases of maize. Adultery with another man's wife or seduction of a man's unmarried daughter is liable in the government court to compensation. Taxes, though a recurrent form of expenditure, may be due during what happens to be a lean period in the life of a family. Other needs may be minor but frequent, and debts accumulate. All these needs must be met in cash.

Whatever the "last straw" contingency is, the sale or pledging of palms and land is the surest way to raise cash quickly. The copra-selling season is a long one occupying most of the year and does not provide the ordinary farmer with any other than a regular income, most of which is used for subsistence. A man obliged to dispose of his property justifies the transaction to his agnates by referring to the immediate need which has befallen his family. This may be no more than a "last straw", and previous expenditure for other needs may have weakened the man's resources. Bearing this in mind, I list in Table 6 the needs which were

TABLE 6. RATIONALE GIVEN BY TSAKANI MEN
FOR SALES OF PALMS AND LAND SINCE 1944.

specified need	number of transactions	specified need	number of transactions
bridewealth	34	expedience*	8
funerals	2	tax	1
sickness	1	compensation	1
debts*	7	emigration	4

*See text for explanation of these terms.

specified as having prompted fifty-eight of the sixty-five transactions since 1944 involving Tsakani men, either as accumulators or losers. I was unable to obtain satisfactory information on the supposed contingencies which gave rise to the remaining seven transactions, all of which occurred in the 1940s.

Whatever else these stated reasons may hide, it is clear that the provision of bridewealth is regarded as the heaviest drain on a person's resources. As mentioned, bridewealth payments are high in relation to the *per-capita* income level.

Funerals and sickness are not cited as frequently as one might expect from observation. However, an investigation of the expenditure in the preceding few years of each of the families which gave debts and expedience as reasons for disposal of property, revealed that eight had been beset by funerals in the preceding two years, while seven had been seeing local doctors for prolonged periods for the treatment of members, three of whom died and so were then given funerals. Two further "expedient" reasons given concerned property which was owned jointly by many brothers but was too small for sub-division. The brothers disputed but could not agree on who among them should buy the property and so agreed to sell it to a non-agnate. Additional reasons for two families were that palms were located too far from the owner's home for him to protect their produce from theft, so he was obliged to sell them. Both families had had a combination of bridewealth, funerary, and local medical expenditure, and these factors were more likely to have prompted the disposal, since it is quite customary to have a nearby relative or friend supervise fragmented and distant holdings. Similarly, the four families who were said to have sold their property because of their migration from the area had previously suffered sickness and death. Indeed, the paramount reasons normally given for moving a home to another area are sickness and death, whether through sorcery or natural misfortune. Bridewealth demands, sickness, and death, then, are the main factors prompting men to dispose permanently of their palms and land.

Conclusion

Although I have explained that bridewealth transactions are the primary means by which the principle of agnation has been upheld, and thereby also the authority of elders to act as witnesses, this is not to say that elders are conscious of the connection. Indeed, in some cases family heads attempt to shirk this responsibility toward a dependent other than a son. But there is a mutually reinforcing circle of sanctions and restraints which obliges older men to perform this duty. As witnesses to the marriage negotiations of other men, their role is to support the custom that bridewealth is given by the groom's family in return for the bride's future offspring, as well as for her domestic and sexual services. By supporting this custom they perpetuate the principle of agnatic membership and entitlement. When the focus shifts to their own homesteads and they are themselves in the position of having to provide for a dependent's bridewealth, they are, however reluctantly, subject to the same sanctions. They are caught in a custom of their own making.

As a further re-inforcement of the system, fathers attempt to acquire bride-wealth on behalf of their own sons before they do so for other dependents. This is stated to be every man's way of strengthening his own family in the years to come, as a means of protecting diminishing family property or of building on that which has been accumulated. It is not surprising, therefore, that as a system of investment the exchange of bridewealth for women and their offspring has been accentuated during the copra boom of the past quarter-century. Rights in women's reproductive powers have become more rigidly defined, and the actual cash value of bridewealth has soared and is no longer payable partly in livestock.

In spite of this accentuation of the cornerstone of agnation, as I have indicated, during the same period less and less property has been transacted between ag-nates. Less property has been transacted between relatives generally, but agnatic ties are now the least useful to an enterprising farmer, since they tend to enable him to acquire only palms, without the land on which they stand.

In this sphere of investment we can say that exchange relations are being phrased more in the idiom of individual contract than of agnation and affinity. At first this sounds like Maine's developmental continuum from status to contract or from ascription to achievement. But it is not this, at all, since it is clear from other societies that kinship is no bar to hard bargaining and contracts. We are dealing with the *idioms* of exchange relations—the way in which such relations are expressed and identified. It is irrelevant that blood ties are less important in initiating contracts. What is important is that people are disputing about the rights and wrongs of selling to non-agnates or non-kinsmen. In disputing about these things, people are expressing an awareness that the capitalist spirit is abroad in their society and that, as far as the losers see it, it threatens the egalitarian, or redistributional, ethos. And once people express this awareness of two fundamentally conflicting principles, they veer to the defence of one principle over the other, according to their circumstantial interests.

However, at this stage of economic development, some common language of custom must remain, in order for enterprising farmers to build up their rival networks of witnesses, informers, and potential sellers of property. This common language of custom is most conveniently that centred on marriage and bride-wealth transactions. It upholds the value of agnation on the one hand, and yet on the other it constitutes by far the greatest contingent expenditure causing poorer men to dispose of their land and palms. Enterprising farmers emphasise this marriage sphere of investment as much as others. This is their contribution, so to speak, to the common language of custom. But in the later period of economic change, as they have become more and more established, they have begun to arrange marriages among themselves. This is most clearly seen in the case of entrepreneurs outside Tsakani as well as within it.

By arranging marriages among themselves, enterprising farmers are able to expect an early total payment of bridewealth for their sisters and daughters and, barring other contingencies, to invest this immediately in the purchase of property. Poorer men also marry their economic equals. But, just as they cannot themselves pay bridewealth immediately for their own wives or for the wives of their sons, so they cannot expect any other than a delayed payment for their own sisters and daughters. Few Giriama bridewealth payments in Kaloleni are protracted beyond five months, so the difference is slight. But it is significant in a situation in which wealth differences are still not great by external, Western standards. It is this investment sphere which I shall next explore.

NOTES

1. In the *Kilifi District Annual Reports* we are told that in 1932 Kaloleni was the most densely populated area in Kilifi District, though still only the third most important cattle-owning location. By 1936 there was specific reference to the "high" copra prices and the "good deal of trade" with the people in Kaloleni and Rabai. And by 1938/1939 it appears that cattle were definitely no longer the dominant subsistence mode, with the closure of ghee dairies early in 1938 and an outbreak of East Coast fever affecting the stock in Kaloleni.

6. Custom Strengthened: Bridewealth

Recent Developments

For at least twenty-five years there have been four parallel developments affecting bridewealth transactions: the monetization of bridewealth; the inflation of bridewealth; a shortening of the time during which bridewealth payments may be completed; and a more rigid definition of the mode by which bridewealth secures rights in a wife's offspring.

Developments of this kind are triggered by precedents. Precedents require discussion and arbitration before they are agreed upon. They are, of course, dealt with by the Giriama elders in their roles as witnesses and mediators in local moots, the government court, and the Mijikenda Union. The fourth development, that is, the more rigid definition of social fatherhood or genetricial entitlement (guardianship rights over a wife's children, regardless of their begetter), goes beyond emphasising a need for mediators. It draws sharp, unambiguous lines of membership between agnatic descent groups and clans and sub-clans. As I have discussed, agnation is the main ideological principle supporting the mediatory roles and, by extension, the ritual roles in the gerontocracy.

These developments therefore oblige the accumulator to continue to seek out the support of his own witnesses in an attempt to justify his claims in the future. But, though this is not recognised by Giriama, these same developments favour the expansionist efforts of the accumulators by facilitating the circulation of increasingly large sums of money. For the solvent farmer whose own subsistence needs are well budgeted for, these sums can be used to purchase palms and land. By contrast, the less fortunate farmer is obliged by custom, for reasons which I shall discuss in Chapter 7, to sell property in order to raise the cash for a male dependent's bridewealth. I shall describe these developments and show how they have facilitated economic differentiation.

The Monetization of Bridewealth

Giriama can point to the famine of the sacks of 1898–1900 as a time when it was still possible to trade only one sack of millet for domestic and sexual rights in a wife; this was followed, but never preceded by, giving some large gourds of millet beer for rights over her reproductive powers. Livestock or cash were in use before 1920 in some parts of Giriamaland, however, for securing sexual and domestic rights, with palm wine displacing millet beer for the genetricial rights. The oldest man in Tsakani acquired his first wife a little while after the Giriama Rising of 1914 by paying her father two rupees when she came to his homestead and two rupees together with the palm wine during the second year of his marriage. Another old Tsakani man paid eight heifers and wine over a period of years at about the same time.

Seventy-four of the eighty-five men of Tsakani are married or have been married at some time. Together, their past and present marriages total one hundred fifty-one. To illustrate the replacement of livestock by cash in Kaloleni, I shall consider information on the composition and amount of bridewealth paid in ninety-nine of these marriages, which represent most of those undertaken by Tsakani men in the Kaloleni area.

Before monetization, bridewealth in Kaloleni could consist of heifers or goats for uxorial rights in the woman, and a bull *(ndzau)* or palm wine for genetricial rights in her. Ten goats seem always to have been equivalent to one heifer, as were two bulls. (In practice only young bulls, that is bullocks, are transacted. Animals are never castrated; cf. Beidelman 1966.) Bridewealth could consist of a mixture of cattle, goats, and money. This mixture would occur when men paid their bridewealth over a few years in different media, as one or another became available.

As Kaloleni yielded its grazing land to the rapidly growing palms, and as money was pumped into the society, first by Asians and later by enterprising Giriama themselves, cash edged out the use of livestock in bridewealth. This monetization has increased dramatically over the past quarter-century (see Table 7).

TABLE 7. LIVESTOCK/CASH COMPOSITION OF BRIDEWEALTH TRANSACTIONS UNDERTAKEN IN KALOLENI BY LIVING TSAKANI MEN.

	all or mostly livestock[1]	roughly equal livestock and cash	all or mostly cash[2]	number of transactions
1920–1929	2 (50%)	1 (25%)	1 (25%)	4
1930–1939	5 (56%)	1 (11%)	3 (33%)	9
1940–1949	5 (38.5%)	0	8 (61.5%)	13
1950–1959	5 (14.7%)	3 (8.8%)	26 (76.5%)	34
1960–mid–1967	2 (5.1%)	3 (7.7%)	34 (87.2%)	39
TOTAL	*19 (19.2%)*	*8 (8.1%)*	*72 (72.7%)*	*99*

1. All but 3 are exclusively livestock.
2. All but 5 are exclusively cash.

The last time that bridewealth in Tsakani consisted exclusively of livestock was in 1960. Since and including that occasion, there have been thirty-nine complete transactions of bridewealth, thirty-four of them exclusively in cash. Looking beyond Table 7, it is interesting to note that a quarter of all exclusively-cash bridewealth transactions since 1957 have been for non-Giriama women, principally of the neighbouring Mijikenda sub-group, the Jibana. Intermarriage among the Mijikenda sub-groups seems always to have occurred, usually in border areas. In Tsakani men explain that the Jibana, who have lived within the palm belt longer than they have, always insist on cash, alone, for bridewealth, with such remarks as "you cannot buy palms with cattle and goats". It is not simply the Jibana who introduced into Tsakani the exclusive use of cash for bridewealth. They, like the Giriama of Kaloleni, have responded to the changing ecological and economic conditions which have made cash expedient and livestock inexpedient.[1] Their common experience points to what must surely be a general process affecting all Mijikenda peoples along the East African coast who have moved from the hinterland and entered an economy centred on palms. Though the scarcity of grazing land for cattle has been the ecological prompter of the switch to cash, the economic usefulness of cash is that surplus bridewealth (bridewealth not needed immediately or at all for the marriage of a male dependent), can be used to buy palms. As the value placed on palms has risen, therefore, there has been a corresponding rise in the value of the increasingly monetized bridewealth. In other words, the Giriama suffer from inflation.[2]

Bridewealth inflation is reported for much of Africa and often has two aspects. One is that the average rate of bridewealth may have risen on an approximate par with the rise in the cost of living. The second is that, additionally or alternatively, a system of graded rates may have emerged, by which the fathers of educated girls expect to be compensated adequately for having invested in their daughters' schooling, and so receive more valuable bridewealth than fathers of uneducated girls. So few Giriama girls of marriageable age have received any schooling that this graded system has not operated among them, though it will surely emerge in the future.

Bridewealth consisting of livestock would comprise between eight and fifteen heifers and a bull "for the children". In Tsakani from about 1920 to 1940 the average was about eight heifers and a bull. From 1940 to 1960 the rate gradually rose to between twelve and fifteen heifers and a bull or its equivalent in palm wine. During both periods an equivalent number of goats was acceptable instead of some of the heifers.[3] Since the price of livestock has itself risen during these years, as has the number of livestock transacted, we can say that more than simply inflation has occurred. There has been an actual increase in the real value of bridewealth.

The monetization of bridewealth has not stopped this increase, as we see by the sixty-seven instances in which only cash has been used (Table 8). The average

TABLE 8. VALUE OF ALL-CASH BRIDEWEALTH PAYMENTS IN TSAKANI
(in Shillings).

	average	median	number of cases
1920–1929	240	———	1
1930–1939	980	600	3
1940–1949	1,000	1,000	7
1950–1959	1,234	1,300	25
1960–mid–1967	1,400	1,425	31

over the past two and a half years has actually risen to 1,511 shillings and in Kaloleni in 1967 a few men paid over 2,000 shillings as bridewealth, a figure reached only once in Tsakani in 1965.

We get the same picture of a steady increase since 1940 when we compare all bridewealth transactions, including those consisting partly or wholly of livestock, as well as those of cash (Table 9). I have converted into cash values by pricing

TABLE 9. AVERAGE CASH VALUE OF BRIDEWEALTH PAYMENTS IN TSAKANI
(in Shillings).

1940–1949	738 (13 payments)
1950–1959	1,216 (35 payments)
1960–1967	1,368 (39 payments)

a heifer at 60 shillings and a goat at 6 shillings up to 1949 and at 100 shillings and 10 shillings, respectively, thereafter until 1967.[4] These are the conversion values used by Giriama and adopted from the tax assessors, even though at present the livestock would cost more at Mariakani market twelve miles from Kaloleni. Since so few livestock are now used as even a part of bridewealth in Tsakani, this is not an important difference.

Shortened Bridewealth Transactions

The quest for palms has been the factor in recent years which has pushed up the value of bridewealth. A rise in the purchase price of palms from 10 shillings to 20 shillings in 1957 was followed by a marked increase in bridewealth costs. There have been associated developments, also. As explained, a wholly-cash bridewealth is useful to accumulators because it can be used, barring other expenses, to purchase palms and land. Its usefulness is enhanced if the accumulator receives the money, if not in one lump sum, then at least within a short time. Similarly, the loser who is obliged to sell palms and land in order to raise the cash to meet some exigency needs the money immediately: he has naturally been loath to dispose of such property until his resources reached a minimum, and now his need is desperate. The two needs balance each other, with the result that protracted payments for palms and land or bridewealth are discouraged by those to whom they are due. Apart from mortgages, which are rarely redeemed, long-standing credit involves much smaller sums—rarely more than one or two hundred shillings.

From a detailed investigation of marriage histories it appears that bridewealth payments were more likely to be drawn out, even for years, when the medium was mostly or wholly livestock.[5] Even in recent years when livestock was occasionally included in bridewealth with cash, it was expected that, after paying the cash portion, a man would delay a year or so in delivering the cattle or goats. With bridewealth now paid wholly in cash, the range of payment is only three to five months. There is an initial payment of about a half at the time the wife is taken to her husband's home. Even this appears to have increased from a third within the past ten years or so.

A short instance may illustrate the pressures to which the fathers of grooms, are increasingly subject: The son of Karisa of Tsakani and the daughter of BiKadzo were to be married. In January 1967, Karisa agreed with BiKadzo on 1,550 shillings bridewealth, 1,050 shillings of which he paid immediately. He was to pay the rest together with the palm wine "for the children" a few weeks later after felling a large number of coconuts and selling the copra prepared from them. They agreed also that the bride would not join her husband until that time. Karisa then had difficulty in hiring young men in the neighbourhood to help his son fell the coconuts. They were occupied elsewhere. Then, when this was at last accomplished, some of the women in the homestead fell sick and for a short time were unable to prepare the copra. It was not until May that Karisa was able to sell sufficient copra to the co-operative to raise the outstanding bridewealth payment. He went immediately to BiKadzo. But BiKadzo told him that he was too late and that he had accepted bridewealth from another man. BiKadzo thereupon returned the 1,050 shillings to Karisa with apologies, explaining that he had needed the money immediately. His daughter apparently had agreed to her father's wishes. Karisa and his witnesses deplored what they considered to be a Jibana influence creeping in among Giriama. They said that a few years previously a man would have done well to have completed the payment within five months. Now it seemed that even that was not enough.

Such harrowing experiences are remarkably similar in this transactional aspect to those arising from the scramble for palms: When Kazungu of Tsakani died, his sons agreed that they should fulfil an obligation to the most junior of them that he should be married. In 1966 they proposed to sell some palms and land to Masha for 1,500 shillings—for the brother's bridewealth. Masha paid 1,000 shillings immediately and promised the rest "next month". After a few weeks he was told that he had been outbid by another man, who had valued the property more highly and had offered the brothers 2,000 shillings. In this case Masha's witnesses saw no cause for complaint; they said simply that this was the way in which men competed for palms, but that it was not the true way of the Giriama, who had not been palm cultivators originally. As in the instance above, we can note how the "blame" for hard, crudely contractual negotiations which disregard men's brotherhood is directed away from some ideal model of traditional Giriama society. This becomes an obvious symbolic weapon in the hands of elders striving to exert their influence.

The interconnectedness of palm and bridewealth transactions is recognised by some Giriama in such statements as: "When I sell palms to get a wife, then that wife is my property. She will help me cultivate and will bear children for me. These children will make a strong family for me. The daughters will [through the bridewealth received for them] enable the sons to marry and have children and will enable me to acquire more palms and more wives." If families were of equal size and had more daughters than sons, and if palms continued to proliferate on unlimited stretches of suitable land, then this ideal might approach reality for many men. As it is, it remains a basic and, in the Giriama context, reasonable ideological justification for many transactions of palms and bridewealth.

Re-defining Paternity

Just as the period of bridewealth payment has been shortened, so there has developed a more rigid definition of how and when genetricial rights in a wife are acquired. In the first instance above, it was agreed that BiKadzo's daughter would not join her husband in his homestead until all the bridewealth and palm wine had been handed over. This does not happen in all cases, but is certainly wide-spread and appears to be increasing. In view of the fact that bridewealth payments are completed within a short period, this extra clause in the contract, so to speak, is practicable. It was impracticable when payments in Kaloleni took longer and is not practised now among hinterland Giriama who continue to use livestock.

The new custom is really a form, pushed to the limits, of a more general development, an alteration of the stage at which the palm wine "for the children" is handed over. Giriama have not abandoned in principle the long-established custom that the palm wine (called the bull) alone secures genetricial rights in a bride. Many years ago the bull would be given to the girls's family early in the protracted bridewealth payments. Even until about ten years ago, the bull would normally be given after about a third or a half of the main bridewealth *(hunda)* had been transacted. But cases occurred which prompted an alteration of the timing: A wife might be made pregnant during the few months between payment of the bull and the remaining bridewealth, but then she and her husband might quarrel and divorce. The bull and portion of bridewealth already paid by the husband would be returned to him; but, since the husband had in fact paid the bull by the time the wife's pregnancy was discovered, he would be entitled to claim the child as his own, subject to making some small maintenance payment to its mother during its early years.

The bull or palm wine is of course of negligible value compared to the cash bridewealth. Giriama recognised this: Why give away valuable children for so little? The practice developed, therefore, of insisting that the groom's father delay payment of the palm wine until all or nearly all the cash bridewealth had been paid. This meant that if, during the few months between the initial and final cash transactions, the bride became pregnant but did not go through with the marriage, then her father could claim that no bull had been paid for the child and therefore he could keep her child within his homestead "as his own". From cases I have recorded, he will only do this if the child is a girl. He or his sons will be entitled to sole rights of use over bridewealth received for her when she eventually marries. His daughter, now divorced from her husband, is free to marry another man.

However, once both bridewealth and the bull have been received by the girl's father, then he is very reluctant that the marriage be dissolved. For by this stage divorce will mean that the girl's father must return the whole bridewealth to the husband, regardless of the number of children born to the husband and now legally his. The Giriama do not reduce returned bridewealth according to the number of children produced by the divorced wife, as do many other Kenya peoples. This means that the girl's father or brothers resist very strongly her attempts to leave her husband. The bridewealth money may have been used to acquire a wife for one of them or to purchase palms, or it may be earmarked for one of these purposes. It cannot easily be returned.

These restraints mean that divorce is much more likely to occur during the early months of a marriage, either before the bull and final bridewealth payment have been made or, at least, even when these have been handed over, before they have been disposed of by the girl's father. Thereafter divorce is much less frequent. This tendency among the Giriama and certain other African societies (like the Fort Jameson Ngoni) for divorce to occur during the first year or two of marriage may raise the overall divorce rate, so that a statistical measure gives the society a high rate of divorce. Yet this high rate may hide the fact that, once beyond a certain initial stage of the marriage, women are under definite pressure to keep the marriage intact, and thereafter the divorce rate is decidedly low.

In advancing his and Mitchell's statistical device for measuring divorce rates, Barnes (1967, p. 93) recognises this confusion. Among Giriama we cannot ignore this feature, since otherwise we are given a wrong impression by the figures, which show them as having only a middle-range divorce rate, when from common-sense observation, as well as from the figures, it is clear that after, say, the birth of her first child, a Giriama woman in Kaloleni is very seldom divorced. In Tsakani, the average duration for thirty-six marriages ended by death was about 14 years. But the average for fifty-three terminated by divorce was only 4.3 years. In only ten of the marriages ending in divorce had children been born.

The present marital status of the adult male population of Tsakani is as follows: 11 unmarried, 69 married, 1 widowed, and 4 divorced. Thus, 74 of the 85 adult males of Tsakani have at some time been married. Information on the marriage history of one of them, currently a monogamist, was unavailable.

Among them, the 69 presently married men have 104 wives with whom they share common *menages*. This excludes three wives, all of one man, who have been separated from their husband for a number of years, but for whom bridewealth has not been reclaimed. These three constitute the only cases of "absolute" separation without divorce, and I regard them as divorcees for present purposes. The current polygyny rate in Tsakani is therefore 104:69, or 1.5.

The marital histories of all 73 ever-married men and 104 women were collected. The only women in Tsakani who have been married but whose complete histories could not be obtained are 11 very old widows. The total number of past and present marriages experienced by the 73 men is 151, while for the 104 women it is 157, of which 30 are unions arising from effective widow inheritance.[6] If we deduct the 104 unions which are common to both men and wives, the total of past and present marriages for the men and women of Tsakani is 204. They encompass about forty years, from about 1927 to 1967, and include 104 existing unions, 53 ended by divorce, and 36 by death.

Following the scheme of Mitchell and Barnes, the divorce rates are:

TABLE 10. DIVORCE RATIOS IN TSAKANI.

ratio	no. in census sample	value
A. Number of marriages ended in divorce, expressed as a percentage of all marriages	53/204	26.0
B. Number of marriages ended in divorce, expressed as a percentage of all marriages completed by death or divorce	53/89	59.5
C. Number of marriages ended in divorce, expressed as a percentage of all marriages except those ended by death	53/164	32.3

Ratios of this kind do not, of course, account for variations in jural and conjugal stability between societies. Giriama conjugal separation, in the conventional sense of marital breakdown, involves a return to the husband of bridewealth and so almost always constitutes technical divorce. Among the Ganda and other Interlacustrine Bantu of East Africa, however, it seems that there is a high separation rate, but a low divorce rate (first reported in Mair 1940). Bridewealth is generally irrecoverable among these people, and so the ex-husband of a broken union will not bother to reclaim it. Nor does it secure for him genetricial rights. The children subsequently born to his wife by other men cannot be claimed by him. Rarely, therefore, is the union formally terminated by a return of bridewealth and so, in this customary sense, rarely involves divorce.

For this reason we can assume that the divorce ratios for Ganda quoted by Mitchell (1967, p. 23) are perfectly correct, as such, but necessarily hide a considerably higher rate of conjugal separation. If this is the case, and if we measure the rate of conjugal separation prompted by marital disharmony rather than the formal divorce rate, then Giriama would have a much lower rate than Ganda. As it is, the Giriama are ranked at the tail end of the patrilineal peoples with relatively low divorce rates as listed by Mitchell, when in fact both their jural and conjugal stability are high after an initial stage in the marriage.

This is relevant for my next step: to show how marriage, and therefore affinal ties, can be regarded by Giriama as potential sources of support. Men who require this support must therefore guide their sisters' and daughters' choices of husbands. Thereafter, these married sisters and daughters must be encouraged to stay with their husbands, lest affinal support be withdrawn. How, then, does the position of women in Giriama society facilitate their being controlled in this way?

The Controls over Women

Cash bridewealth, its rising value, a shortened period for payment, and a sharpening of its negotiable value in securing genetricial rights, are clearly results of the recent economic consequences of a switch to marketing copra and coconuts more than palm wine. Yet, in the manner of a feed-back system, these developments have facilitated further economic differentiation by making possible the circulation within the society of large sums of money which can be invested in the purchase of palms by an enterprising few.

We can go further to say that Giriama marriage represents, among other things, an economic and social investment. This is a familiar enough phenomenon, which is as characteristic of elite in-marrying in modern industrial society as it is of some pre-industrial communities. The bridewealth is now in Kaloleni an economic asset consisting of cash, which can be used to acquire either more wives for an agnatic family or more palms for an individual. The social investment entailed in marriage is the support of affines, either as witnesses or as distributors of profitable information.

The low divorce and separation rates afford a protection to these investments. They are made possible by restricting four sets of choices and activities open to a woman. First, there are very few ways in which she can earn money for her own independent use. Second, she may choose her husband, but only from among approved suitors living within her father's neighbourhood. Third, and similarly, she may choose the replacement for her deceased husband, but with suggestions by clan elders. Fourth, even in the ritual sphere, any powers she may acquire are limited; for instance, she is not normally credited with the power to practise sorcery or to become a traditional doctor, while even as a diviner her work may be to diagnose and to recommend a doctor (who is male and whose earnings from the patient greatly exceed hers).

All of these restrictions may be said to reflect male control of women's activities. Giriama is not an isolated society. As mentioned, a very few Giriama women become Muslim and, by working in Mombasa, repay their own bridewealth and thus secure independent status. There are two cases in Tsakani of wives having "run off" to Mombasa to do this, and there are a few cases in Kaloleni. This is not to say that Giriama women express dissatisfaction with their status. Such sentiments would be difficult to measure reliably. But for men the fact that such escape is possible is a frequent topic and an apparent cause of concern. Both in jest and seriously, they dispute the wisdom of giving women more "freedom".

More specifically, women's limited economic opportunities and the tendency to choose their spouses from nearby families are the two key features which enable Giriama marriage to operate as an investment system. Economically, first, it is possible, without imposing ethnocentric judgements, to say that the opportunities available to women to make independent choices of action are indeed restricted.

In the open areas of Giriamaland beyond the palm belt, a wife or co-wife is entitled to her own garden *(koho)*, in which she can grow crops to be used as she pleases, provided she has done her share of cultivation in the main garden *(munda)* worked by all wives together. With the extension of the palm belt in Kaloleni, little land is available for any other than this larger "husband's garden". In Tsakani, figures show that, as the numbers of palms and people have increased, fewer new wives have been allocated their own gardens. Crops from the communal main garden are in no way the property of an individual wife and are used either for subsistence or as the husband or his homestead head determines. Copra, as a new crop, has always been the prerogative of men, who determine the use of cash earned from selling it. This is also the case with other even more recent tree crops such as citrus fruits and cashew nuts.

Older Giriama women may earn small sums from making and selling brooms and palm thatches for house roofs, and a few female diviners earn a little; but these are meagre sources of income. Mothers receive no portion of the cash bridewealth given for their daughters, as they do among many other peoples having an agnatic house-property complex. Few Giriama women are educated and, except for some of the very few Muslims, do not work anywhere for wage-labour.

A woman's ineffectual economic status, transacted rather than transacting, mirrors the second restriction placed upon her, namely, her acceptance of a husband from within her father's neighbourhood or his range of local contacts. Again, figures show that as Tsakani's population increased and became more settled, more marriages occurred within a few miles' radius.

The Political Significance of Neighbourhood and Affinity

The Giriama explain the preference for local endogamy[7] by stressing how important it is to know the characters of a girl and her mother and whether they have been victims of such believed-to-be contagious or hereditary diseases as leprosy, tuberculosis, and asthma, or whether they are suffering from the ritually polluting effects of a supernatural affliction (*kirwa* or *mavingano*), which causes the sickness and death of children. Friendship between families is thus an excellent pre-condition for the marriage between them of a son and a daughter. This is a reversal of the sentiment typically expressed by peoples with widely ramifying lineage systems, such as Luo and Nuer, or the Mae-Enga (Meggit 1965) in New Guinea, who claim to marry among people whom traditionally they would fight.

Thus, neighbourhood ties are potential ties of affinity. More than this, the Giriama have a remarkable system of serial linking through affines. That is to say, a man may get to know and have relations not only with his affines, but also with their affines, and with the affines of the latter, and so on. Funerals are the great public occasions when these links are most used and publicised. Funeral ceremonies are always attended by hundreds of people, recruited through the system of serial linking through affines, who reciprocate past obligations to each other by contributing food and palm wine to the ceremonies.

At one level, funeral ceremonies may be said to reconcile discrepant principles of organisation in the society. This is a familiar function of collective ceremonies already well described for many societies. At a second level, these ceremonies, which are frequent and last many days and nights, may be said to constitute stock-markets of influence. That is to say, they are public occasions advertising the current state of relations between family heads: Are they seen talking earnestly together, perhaps bargaining or clinching deals, or are they conspicuously aloof from each other? More than simply advertising current relations between family heads, the occasions are long enough for new ties to be forged and old ones broken, perhaps with the excuse of a quarrel.

There are general similarities here to the situation described by Barth for Swat Pathan, among whom large-scale rites of passage are occasions for expressing alliance or enmity. I shall discuss these similarities in illustrating the sociological significance of Giriama funerals in Chapter 7. For the moment, it is relevant to consider precisely what kinds of marriage, and therefore affinal choices, are made by the men of Tsakani. It is then necessary to see how their choices are affected by the value of bridewealth as a possible economic investment and by its value in providing affines who may act as witnesses or informers, but who are more likely to provide contacts of this kind through their own serially linked affines.

Giriama society has always had its wealthy men. Their wealth might earlier have consisted of cattle or control over palm wine, and so have been restricted in scale by technical and ecological factors. Polygyny was and is prized by such men, where they still exist, as a symbol of their eminence. Typically, they would marry the daughters of poorer men at the request of the latter, who would thereafter be supporters. The important point is that the wealth of such men was invested not in limitless numbers of palms or cattle, but in acquiring large numbers of wives and thus children. A former chief of Kaloleni is an interesting example of one who was undoubtedly economically successful as a cattle farmer and trader in palm wine, but who invested nearly all his wealth in wives. He retired from the chiefship in 1957, died in 1965, and left behind him a considerable estate but such a large family that the inheritance due to each son was not above the average of that received by sons of much less wealthy farmers. This is an extreme example. But at lesser levels the custom might have operated thus: A needy supplicant might request a wealthy man to take his daughter in marriage as a means of acquiring bridewealth for the marriage of one of his sons. The wealthy man thereby would acquire political support as well as a wife, but he also would dispose of capital, which in more modern times might have been used to purchase palms for the production and marketing of copra and coconuts. He therefore operated within a primarily re-distributional rather than capitalist economy, as I have defined these terms.

Most of the losers in Tsakani have two or three wives each, some of whom have been acquired in this way, even recently. A few of the accumulators also may well have directed their resources too much in this direction. Time will tell. Controlling for age differences, the rate of polygyny among accumulators is not significantly different from that among losers. The main difference is that within the past twelve years most of the accumulators have tended to marry the daughters not of poorer, needy supplicants, but of prosperous men like themselves. This trend seems marked in the case of seven accumulators and their male dependants. In the wider context of Kaloleni, also, established entrepreneurs marry into high-status families like their own.

In other words, as the copra-based economy has furthered economic differentiation, and as enterprising farmers have emerged to take advantage of the new economy in the favourable conditions of a boom in prices and later of political independence, men have tended to marry the daughters of economic equals. There are fewer and fewer cases of poorer men's daughters' marrying into richer families. Once again, this is a familiar phenomenon in many societies which are stratified into economic and social groups or categories. In Kaloleni, however, this differentiation of status groups is still developing. The only two "cultural" features distinguishing the accumulators from the losers, apart from their agricultural techniques and ambitions, are their women's dress, which tends to be Western instead of the Giriama cotton skirt *(hando)* and wrap, and their greater investment in children's education. All other common customs are retained. As explained, this common language of custom is still needed as a means by which accumulators can acquire witnesses and informers from among the losers and thus continue to expand their holdings of palms and land.

Marriage into the families of economic equals means that specific pairs of accumulators are affines to each other. The accumulators are in competition with each other and therefore are rivals. But this does not mean that the two fathers of a couple or a father- and son-in-law or two brothers-in-law engage in open competition for a single plot of palms which is for sale. Nor is a man who is affine to two contenders for palms expected to take sides. Giriama are fully aware of who is married to whom and make allowances for such delicate situations of conflicting loyalties and obligations. There thus must be situational selectivity in the recruitment of witnesses to a transaction or dispute or in the creation of an information network. This is why any one enterprising farmer has to have a network of witnesses who are diversely recruited. They are thus likely to be loose-knit, in terms of their own relations with each other, to begin with. And, as suggested, they should be kept loose-knit by the farmer, lest he be faced by an organised core of witnesses who demand amounts of patronage which exceed his resources. A witness may himself be linked to one or more other enterprising farmers, so he, too, must exercise selectivity in siding with one farmer rather than another.

There is an analytical distinction of some importance to be made here. There are societies in which factions may come to involve fairly unambiguous loyalties and close-knit memberships and are in a sense proto-corporate groups (cf. Nicholas 1965, p. 28, and Bailey 1969, p. 53). But in Kaloleni the network of witnesses centred on a farmer operates most efficiently for him when he can have regular but not close relations with only a few witnesses independently and can rely on each of them to act as broker by recruiting known aides, when needed. Such action-sets, as they have been called (A. C. Mayer 1966 and Gulliver 1971), can thus be said to arise from a situation in which an ambiguity in loyalties and group membership actually facilitates an emerging economic differentiation which has not yet given birth to a system of stratified corporate groups.

However, an enduring cleavage is developing. It is not visible or openly expressed at the level of neighbouring homesteads, where the common language of custom must prevail. It shows itself periodically at the level of the Kaloleni trading centre during major events involving a large number of persons who are not necessarily bound to each other in the face-to-face obligations of neighbouring homesteads. Examples of such events during 1966 and 1967 were a national anti-sorcery movement (see Parkin 1968 and 1970), a series of disputes centring on the local farmers' co-operative, county council elections, and a celebrated court case involving the most famous Giriama entrepreneur and his paternal uncle. It is at these events that accumulators veer toward defence of one principle and losers, mainly elders, toward defence of a contrary one (see Chapter 7).

The choice by accumulators to marry into the families of fellow accumulators is an aspect of this developing cleavage. This can be seen in at least two benefits derived from this status-group endogamy. First, bridewealth transacted between them tends to be paid more quickly than average. If your daughter marries an accumulator or his son, then you are unlikely to wait long before you have the lump sum. It is considered shameful for a man of means to prolong bridewealth payments "like a pauper". You can thus time an eligible daughter's marriage into an accumulator's family to make it possible to work quickly on information that a plot of palms is coming up for sale. Second, though accumulators compete for the purchase of palms, close affines are exempt from this competition with each other and may actually provide mutual support in the moot or government court when faced by a claimant and his witnesses. They do not help each other only for charity, however. Rather, they expect that help will be reciprocated in future predicaments.

I move now to consider how the common language of custom is expressed at funerals which nonetheless constitute the stock-markets of influence in which support is acquired, retained, and assessed.

NOTES

1. F. R. Wilson, District Commissioner, Kilifi, reports in 1949 a contrast between cattle and cash payments in "pastoralist" and "non-pastoralist" areas. "Notes on Bride Price". *Kilifi District Annual Report,* 1949.

2. Moving outside the immediate area of my fieldwork, we see a linkup of all these factors in the

following general reference from the 1952 *Kilifi District Annual Report,* under the heading "African Courts": "There is a noticeable predominance of litigation in the southern locations where the population is most dense and where there are therefore greater human problems. Land cases are on the slight increase and there is widespread resistance to accepting the return of dowry [*sic,* but meaning bridewealth] in cash, or in the cash value of cattle, rather than in cattle themselves. This is due to the conscious and established [official] policy of controlling the tendency for dowry payments to increase and is effected by fixing a court value on the price of stock which remains constant, and considerably below the open market price". From my figures and life histories it is clear that people in Tsakani coped with this new problem by asking for a cash bridewealth in the first place and incidentally thereby eluding the administration's attempt to curb bridewealth inflation.

3. Again, more generally, Wilson (1949) writes that in 1949 Giriama bridewealth rates were either 70 to 85 goats (five of them male) or 7 heifers and a bull, or 500 shillings and palm wine.

4. In 1966 the Kaloleni government court started to assess the value of a heifer at 150 shillings.

5. F.R. Wilson (1949) reports that, as early as the late forties, both cash and stock were "normally" paid in one instalment. But he appears to be making a general reference to all Mijikenda in Kilifi District and could therefore be ignoring local variations in the rate at which this occurred.

6. In what I call effective widow inheritance the widow moves to reside permanently in the homestead of her new husband, whom she has chosen and who will be regarded as legal father of any children subsequently born to her. Such widows are still of child-bearing age. In nominal widow inheritance such a widow does not reside in her new "husband's" homestead. She is past child-bearing age. The union is consummated in the widow's homestead, in which she continues to live. Thereafter she may see her husband only when he visits her at intervals, sometimes of many months. In assessing the number of separate marriages, I ignore these jural but non-conjugal unions, which number fifteen.

7. The Luo of Kenya, to take one example, have a high degree of lineage and clan localisation and disallow any form of cousin marriage. They frequently prefer to marry women from other than their natal locations. In contrast to Giriama, they have no preference for local endogamy. Among Giriama within the palm belt, the homesteads of many exogamous clans are interspersed within the more densely populated areas. Matrilateral cross-cousin marriage is permitted. These factors facilitate a wide range of choice of spouse from among neighbouring homesteads without transgressing the rules of clan exogamy.

7. Custom Strengthened: Funerals

The Mortuary Ceremony as a Major Event

Funerals among Giriama have two broad aspects. One is the familiar one of bringing together people who in other contexts are opposed and, through the use of symbolic motifs, of obliging them—at least ostensibly—to reconcile their differences. I say "ostensibly" because, during the course of the funeral, many participants use the occasion to assess the social standing of their rivals or of possible supporters, and to advertise their own. A second aspect of the funeral, therefore, is that it provides an opportunity for men to display their worthiness as possible supporters of accumulators or as buyers or mortgagees of palms and land. In other words, the occasion is an opportunity for the organization of social credit, played out under an umbrella of communal amity.

Among the Swat Pathan, as described by Barth (1959), weddings seem to have the status that funerals do among Giriama. Each is the most significant rite of passage in its society. Both are occasions which are organised on a neighbourhood basis, but which also draw in agnates, affines, and other kin. They are occasions which, among the Swat Pathan, attract high and low caste and political overlord and follower, and among Giriama, similarly draw together accumulators and losers.

From Barth's material on the weddings and other rites of passage, it is possible to list the following six characteristics: 1. the basic one, food and services are reciprocated by the sponsors of different ceremonies, though rich and poor households are not expected to contribute the same amounts (pp.32–33); 2. the ceremonies are public and are well attended (p.31); 3. "the scale of the ceremonies is roughly commensurate with the rank and wealth of the household of the person for whom they are held" (p.32); 4. there is something of a "moral" compulsion to attend on those eligible to do so (p.33); 5. those who dodge this expectation thereby advertise their enmity with central figures around whom or by whom the ceremony is organised (p.41); and 6. the ceremony gives men the chance to establish political ties, sometimes through arranging marriages (p.41).

These six features characterise Giriama funerals, as well. However, there is a striking difference between the Swat Pathan and Giriama situations. Swat chiefs spend recklessly in providing hospitality and in sponsoring ceremonies. Barth writes that this potlatch-like development "only seems intelligible if we recognise that the underlying motives are political rather than economic" (p.12). This is perhaps what we might expect of a basically re-distributional economy. Among Giriama, however, their conversion of lavish hospitality into political support was more characteristic of the time when livestock and grain were used for bride-wealth and when land did not have the exchange value conferred on it by palms, or later when palm wine was the major trading commodity. As mentioned, at that time a rich man might marry the daughter of a poor man in order to help him and thereby earn his support. But, when the cash economy based on copra developed, such use of bridewealth for acquiring a wife, rather than palms, made the man a poor starter in the scramble for palms.

Nowadays, it is not accumulators, or even established entrepreneurs, who spend recklessly. They certainly sponsor lavish funerals. But, as is clear if one listens to one of them discuss the matter with his witnesses, they calculate very carefully how lavish their sponsorship should be. Does the death of *X* merit the provision of one or two bulls, and how many goats and how much palm wine?

Swat chiefs seem preoccupied with acquiring political support at all costs. By contrast, Giriama accumulators and entrepreneurs seek support and contacts leading to further wealth at what they calculate to be minimal costs. They keep the economic, as well as political, factors in mind.

It is, in fact, the losers who may be said to spend recklessly, though much less lavishly than the accumulators. They spend recklessly because they will sell almost the last of their palms in order to raise the cash to sponsor an ample funeral for a homestead member. As homestead heads who are likely to be important elders, they are expected to advertise their seniority by honouring the deceased man. The younger accumulators are similarly bound to advertise their reputations—in their case, as generous men. Thus, as among Swat Pathan and in many other societies, notions of honour, or prestige *(ishima)* and shame *(haya)* are used to justify such expenditure, which nevertheless drains the resources of ordinary families. However, there is a crucial difference between the consequences of these notions among Giriama and Swat Pathan. However much land they have, in the end, Swat chiefs have nothing in which to invest their wealth except political support. They can overspend their resources and fall from power (pp.11–12). Giriama accumulators are lodged more firmly on an entrepreneurial ladder. They invest their money in more palms and land. This investment links them inextricably with a national and international market and inevitably offers state protection to the most established of them. The Giriama funeral ceremonies, therefore, have to be viewed as playing a part in a more enduring process of economic differentiation, which is determined ultimately by factors operating outside Giriama society. The funeral ceremonies do this by bringing together people of different and sometimes opposed social categories who nevertheless use the occasion to advertise their availability as witnesses or as buyers and sellers of property.

The huge attendances at funeral ceremonies, frequently by hundreds of persons, is explained by Giriama to be the result of the process whereby an affine, relative, friend, or neighbour of the deceased will invite certain of his own affines to the funeral. They, in turn, will invite certain of their affines, and so on to include, as in one instance which I counted, as many as four serial links or five families. In most cases there are no more than two links involving three families. Most people are drawn from the surrounding area of the deceased's homestead, but a substantial minority are from outlying areas. Both nearby and far-off visitors at funerals include a large proportion whose presence is justified on the basis of affinity or affinal serial linking. As may be obvious, in a small-scale society nearly everyone who is not directly related may be said at least to be a serially linked affine. A man may display or seek support by tracing and discovering such links, as he can with more immediate affinal, agnatic, and cognatic ties. In an area of fairly high population density and a high mortality rate, funerals are frequent and so provide almost regular opportunities for creating and furbishing such ties.

Altogether thirty funerals involving almost twice that number of ceremonies in and around the area of Tsakani came to my attention during my twelve months of fieldwork. Additionally, full burial ceremonies were held for two young children, which is not customary and is said to be a recent development. Both were given to me as examples of the escalatory nature of competition for prestige between homestead heads.

I would like to have obtained a systematic assessment of the proportion of time spent by the adults of Tsakani at funeral ceremonies. This was not possible, but I have estimated that at any one of the thirty funerals (excluding the two for the children) no less, and frequently more, than 75 percent of the 209 adults of Tsakani attended at least parts of the two ceremonies. With the burial ceremony extending over six or seven days and nights and the end-of-mourning ceremony taking up three days and nights, even a day's and a night's attendance at each would ensure regular interaction among the same people at the same formal event and their common exposure to the symbolic or normative themes regularly proclaimed through its activities. In fact, depending on their closeness to the deceased, men and women may spend much more than one day and one night at a ceremony.

The important point here is to indicate that funerals are a major feature of Giriama social organization. They cannot simply be labelled as just another ritual. Any sociological analysis of the Giriama must include them, but it may well exclude consideration of such other individual rites of passage as births and weddings, which involve fewer people, less time, and much less lavish hospitality, and which are really the subject for more specifically focused analyses. Funeral ceremonies are central to Giriama activities in a way that other ceremonies are not. Even during the height of the planting season, people fulfil the minimal obligations of attendance and participation.

Age, Sex, and Conspicuous Consumption

I attended sometimes a whole, but usually only a part of twenty of these funerals. Inevitably, the differing capacities in which I attended gave me varying degrees of access to specific information on how each was organized. Organizers whom I knew well would reveal more details of the natures of decisions taken and the manner in which they were reached than those whom I knew less well. But three aspects are deliberately made public knowledge. One is the identities of men who have contributed palm wine and livestock for sacrifice at the funeral. This advertises men's economic worth. Another is the demarcation of groups at the funeral who will be allocated specific portions of meat and palm wine. This advertises the division between those socially designated as elders and as young men, and the social division between men and women. A third aspect is the demarcation and encouraged competition of rival dancing groups from the surrounding area. As well as exhibiting neighbourhood rivalries, this also denotes generational and sexual divisions and allows for licensed competition between them. Generational and sexual distinctions are also evident in the formal rules of the ceremonies. But beneath the veil of formality, individual competitiveness creeps in.

As mentioned, the Giriama have a first and a second funeral. The first funeral includes the burial and lasts seven days and nights for a man, and six for a woman. The second funeral is held not less than one and not more than four months afterward. It lasts, effectively, three days and nights and is specifically concerned with the appointment of a new homestead head, if necessary, and, in the funeral of a property holder, the appointment of heirs to his property and widows. The days of the first funeral are counted from the day of the actual burial. Should the death occur in the morning, the deceased will be buried in the afternoon; if after midday, then the following morning. Very old people, including women, are buried on the day after death, regardless of the time when they died. These are some of the more obvious differences of age and sex which are expressed in the rules of the ceremony. We shall see more of these two sets of differences and their co-existence as symbolic motifs with the brasher but complementary symbolism of prestige competition.

Before the body is buried, money (called Midzichenda) is collected for the purpose of buying calico cotton for the shroud, wooden planks for the coffin, palm wine for immediate and later consumption, and other items. The term *Midzichenda* is a creation of leading elders of the nine "tribes" of coastal Kenya who, from the 1940s onward, felt a need to express their cultural similarity and common origins and therefore established formal associations. These were manifestly welfare-oriented but served also as informal political platforms and certainly fostered a more unitary consciousness among the nine tribes. The two most important associations were the Mabodze-Madzezi Union and its successor—still strong at the time of writing—the Midzichenda (or *Mijikenda* in Swahili) Union. In this and many other contexts, *Midzichenda* is a term which connotes solidarity. At funerals it thus refers to the money given for the purpose of making the above purchases and is actually said by Giriama to demonstrate the solidarity of persons variously recruited or invited on the basis of the otherwise logically distinct principles of agnation, affinity, and neighbourhood. Yet, even here, men are expected to contribute in full public view as generously as they are able.

Immediately when the body is buried, there is a collective crescendo of wailing, which has hitherto been confined to individual relatives and friends for a short time after each has arrived at the homestead of the deceased. Dancing, drumming, drinking, sacrifice, and meat-eating commence in turn at various points within the following few days. Throughout the first funeral, in the dancing, in the drinking and eating groups, and in the playing of certain stereotyped roles, there is strict segregation of the sexes and a somewhat blurred but discernible segregation of older and younger men. Within each of these categories there is prestige competition. But also—and this is important—rivalry is expressed between categories.

The enjoyment of drinking, eating, dancing, and, more generally, of prestige competition, is not in any way seen to conflict with the recognition that the funeral is a tragic occasion called to mark the loss of a member of the community. The seclusion of the bereaved person or persons and the full view he is given of the ceremonial events are said to have the dual function of respecting his grief and at the same time distracting him from morbid contemplation. (Note here that rites of passage among Swat Pathans are known as *gham-khādi*—'sorrow-happiness'—Barth 1959, p. 31.)

One obvious source of distraction is the expectation that the bereaved (*mfererwa*, sometimes described as the one who sits on the mat and orders) should provide an ample contribution of palm wine and cattle and/or goats for consumption at the funeral. Not even he is exempted from the demand that honour be satisfied. Close relatives and neighbour-friends are also expected to contribute generously. At least two bullocks and a few goats should be provided by the bereaved and others close to the deceased. Otherwise, there would be insufficient meat, and the families responsible would be deprecated. A successful funeral ceremony evokes such comments as *"ni mulume iye"* ('he really is a man') and expressions of the sentiment that the bereaved, who is either the existing homestead head or is likely to be the new one, has been "able to control the homestead in any way, even when a funeral comes".

From observation it is clear that the fear of falling afoul of deprecatory gossip by appearing either mean or, by implication, a poor economic manager, does drive men to attempt to preserve their honour by almost any method. Cash may be raised by mortgaging or selling almost the last of a family's palms and land. Only a minority of the funeral ceremonies coming to my attention had less than the minimum expenditure just mentioned.

Since accumulators, including the entrepreneurs, frequently marry from families similarly placed economically, funerals in their homesteads incur much more lavish contributions from both the bereaved and their affines than do funerals of

A young lead singer performs at a funeral dance, a major occasion for the expression of intergenerational and sexual rivalries. The frequent funerals, often attended by hundreds, are central to the maintenance and formation of social and economic ties among Giriama.

losers. Thus, the funeral cermonies at which accumulators are, or stand in the position of, the bereaved involve larger expenditure on bulls and goats than do those conducted by bereaved losers. The average contribution for each funeral ceremony for accumulators is 2.5 bulls and 11.6 goats, compared to 1.2 bulls and 4.5 goats for losers. Additionally, during my fieldwork two losers actually failed to hold second funerals, in each case on grounds of poverty. No accumulator failed to hold a second funeral.

Accumulators are not only the most able to hold lavish funerary ceremonies for deceased agnates and wives but, in doing so, they establish a model of ideal ceremonial generosity. In honouring their dead they proclaim their own economic substance. Losers never fail to have at least the first funeral. Though in most cases their contributions fall below the minimal ideal of two bulls, the expenditure is frequently a hardship.

Among both accumulators and losers, the bereaved and his agnates contribute the greatest proportion of bulls and goats, but affines make large contributions also. Neighbours who are neither agnates nor affines bring gourds of palm wine to the funeral and may compete with each other in the lavishness of their supplies, inviting to their sides those whose wine is finished or those who have never been able to bring any.

This ethos of unselfishness or sharing is essentially that expressed in the disapproval of accumulators who "relentlessly" expand their holdings of palms and land. But the accumulators can at least compensate for these "moral" shortcomings by seeming to exaggerate to a sometimes remarkable degree their acceptance of the normative value of lavish funerary ceremonies, even though in fact they calculate their contributions carefully. Through the use of particular symbolic motifs funeral ceremonies constantly proclaim the importance of two main normative rules: intergenerational and sexual divisiveness. The accumulators who are generous providers at funerals of agnates or affines, are thus seen to uphold these Giriama ideals. This is the view of Giriama themselves: the accumulators are taking much of the land and trees but at the frequent, lengthy, and lavish funerals they partially redeem themselves.

The main normative themes are intergenerational and sexual divisiveness. They are presented to a congregation which is fairly regular in composition and in the frequency of its interaction and consistent in its expectations of the event. The congregation consists, moreover, of persons variously bound to each other outside the event and in the normal course of social life by ties of affinity, agnation, or neighbourhood, and, in all of these, by actual or potential ties of an economic contractual nature, as accumulator to accumulator, loser to loser, or loser to accumulator and vice versa.

The theme of sexual divisiveness can be said to parallel the restricted nature of women's status, as described.[1] The theme of intergenerational divisiveness goes further than correspondence with the social reality. It subsumes within it the cleavage between losers and accumulators, who tend to be the older and younger family heads, respectively. An approved, or traditional, theme thus legitimates a subversive one.

Intergenerational Conflict as a Subliminal Theme

In the old days a homestead head would never be a young man, but a mature man who used his wisdom to keep his younger brothers and his sons and their wives united and within the same homestead. The homesteads were larger then, and all would respect the head. Only older men practised sorcery. And when they did so, they often had good reason to: younger men of the homestead or outsiders might be trying to bring disunity into the homestead and so had to be quashed. At funerals there was none of this boasting among heads that you get nowadays. Big men who died were respected by the slaughtering of many beasts, but people contributed only what they could afford. The poor were not blamed for contributing little or nothing. At these ancient funerals, only old men were allowed to carry the corpse from its house to the grave. Old men would organise the funeral, and young men were there to take orders. Nowadays young men carry the corpse and do most of the organising.

This reminiscence of an ordered though probably idealised past was given me by a man in his eighties, the oldest man in Tsakani. It includes sentiments echoed many times by other elders and undoubtedly parallels ideal views of the past in other subsistence societies.

It would be very difficult to determine to what extent such pronounced

geronotocratic themes ran through Giriama society's social and ritual organisation. The important term and concept *rika* (age-grade), the alternate generational
naming system of clans and the practice of designating adults by children's and
grandchildren's names are all that remain of a past system of age-organization.
Homesteads are no longer large, except in the cattle zones of the Giriama hinterland. But those who are depicted as sorcerers do tend to be men at least in their
forties and more frequently in their fifties and older. Traditional doctors also tend
to be men well above average in age, while the social effectiveness and importance,
even at the government court level, of *mbari* (clan elders) and of the Mijikenda
Union in solving problems of inheritance, land tenure, marriage, and adultery
compensation ensure continued prominence to roles which only elders play.

But the last sentence in the elder's reminiscence suggests either a completely
reversed situation or a rationalisation of an event like the funeral, whose success
seems to be judged almost completely in terms of its lavishness. For it is certainly
true that younger men carry the corpse to the grave. It is they who walk, often
many miles outside the palm belt, to choose, haggle for, purchase, and finally pull
the required number of bulls to the deceased's homestead. The man who provides
a beast technically has the right to decide at what time of the day and at which
spot and by whom the beast is to be slaughtered. Since the accumulators provide
the most beasts and since they tend to be younger homestead heads, here again
younger men are seen to occupy a more central role than elders. It is in the
allocation of meat and drink and in the provision of comfortable and, during the
day, shady places at which to sit that elders are appeased. And, at the end of the
second funeral *(nyere za mwezi)* it is the elders who constitute a majority on the
mbari council which advises or decides on the allocation of heritable property and
widows. The council rarely numbers fewer than ten and sometimes as many as
twenty-five men.

Dance teams of young men and women compete with each other but, at the
switch to certain changes of tune and rhythm, have to fade from the scene while
older men and women dance and monopolise attention for a short while.

Throughout the funeral ceremony, elders fulfil the expectation that they should
grumble at the "delay" in the slaughter of beasts or in the preparation of food,
or complain at the inadequacy of the palm wine or meat. They bark orders,
usually politely unheeded, at the younger organisers throughout the burial and
afterward.

The funeral is also the time for the "game" of placing persons according to
adjacent-generational seniority. Older and, by this time, inebriated men announce
to the world in harsh tones that so-and-so is their son or son-in-law and "prove"
this by referring to their respective clan names, from which, ideally, generational
seniority can be gauged. They may score points of approval from other elders if
this recitation of and deduction based on clan names is regarded as correct and
if the victim is clearly junior in years as well as, putatively, in generation. But an
approving elder may himself suffer the indignity of being challenged by a young
man of his clan, who by the same technique demonstrates that the older man,

though his senior in years, is of a junior generation, according to the clanship naming system. No doubt, rival elders enjoy seeing each other cut down to size by younger men. But the idiom in which the game is played is that of opposition between old and young.

Though the grumbling, mock complaints and teasing are no more than banter, they emphasise an idealised division between age and youth, which in reality cannot refer to clearly delineated categories. Let me give an instance of what this distinction means and how blurred it is in practice. In Tsakani there is an accumulator who has just turned forty and who is the leader of the most prominent neighbourhood dancing team of young men. He has held this position for nearly ten years. The next oldest team member is in his early thirties. The dance leader, as well as being an accumulator able to boast a successful farm and the possession of many palms, is also called in to arbitrate on affairs of his clan in his area. He sits on his clan council with elders. Physically, he is one of the strongest men in the neighbourhood and continues the profession of tapper, which originally provided the cash with which he accumulated palms. He is only bettered in the number of palms he can tap in a day by one other man in the neighbourhood. He is head of the third largest homestead in the area and has three wives and eight children.

Membership in the dancing teams connotes youthful strength and virility. At the first funeral the teams dance for up to six or seven nights and days, with short breaks for sleep, food, and drink. At night individual members may slip away from the dance and initiate or continue love affairs with young women, usually dancing partners, at a little distance from the homestead, eventually returning to the team. Clearly, membership in the dancing team requires considerable stamina and is one of the most obvious activities dividing those defined as young from old people. The leader of the prominent Tsakani dancing team is too strong physically not to continue as leader but too obviously senior, in terms of the number of wives and children he has and in the size of his homestead, not to be invited onto his clan council. Significantly, he plays a fairly passive role on the council. He is, in short, a good illustration of how blurred is the actual line dividing the idealised categories of old and young and so is able to straddle them both. I shall return to him as an example of how an accumulator must acquire the support of older witnesses and informers by emphasising a common language of custom.

The banter between those defined situationally as young and old refers by innuendo to the ideological conflict between accumulators and losers. On the one hand, the whole system of funeral expenditure is one of several factors prompting the circulation of cash and the disposal of palms and land by poor men in need to those who are ready to buy. On the other hand, the frequent and successive funerals within a small area emphasise a common sense of obligation to attend, participate, and contribute, and so bring together persons who are recruited to the occasion—sometimes by each other—on the basis of ties of agnation, affinity, and neighbourhood.

In so far as these ties of affinity and agnation involve mutual obligations couched in moral tones, the differences dividing accumulators and losers are, for the occasion and on the surface, rendered less immediately apparent. In other words, members of the congregation are supposed to behave toward each other as neighbours, kin or affines, and not as accumulators and losers. And these are ties which involve the generational differences about which people customarily joke and play.

At the risk of a teleological explanation, it can be suggested that the theme of intergenerational conflict at the funeral ceremony deflects attention from or, more properly, "smothers" the burning issue of a growing cleavage between accumulators and losers. Putting this another way, we might say that the growing but unstoppable cleavage between accumulators and losers is expressed subliminally in the more customarily acceptable theme of intergenerational conflict.

This, then, would appear to be yet another function of the funeral ceremony. The pronounced thematic concern with the conflict of adjacent generations is seen to explain more than just that conflict alone. It is also a subliminal mechanism which couches in an expressed customary conflict a much more divisive and non-customary one.

NOTES

1. I intend to devote a full paper to sexual symbolism among Giriama in view of the interesting recent work by Beidelman (1966 and elsewhere).

8. Beyond the Power of Elders

The Politics of Homestead and Nation

In the preceding chapters I have shown how national political and economic changes, which characterise many other Third World countries as well as Kenya, have brought about in Kaloleni a radical redistribution of economic opportunity and entitlement. My analysis has concentrated on the role-conflicts experienced at an interpersonal level among people who interact in the face of two contradictory principles: the local authority system is essentially gerontocratic and in its important judicial aspect is supported by the government court, whereas recent economic opportunities have brought about new sources of influence which are available to younger, enterprising men at early stages of their careers.

It is clear that the new sources of influence have been held in abeyance, so to speak, at the level of homesteads. Enterprising farmers subscribe with other men to a common language of custom which is largely unchanged in its form, but they have radically altered its consequences: Bridewealth and funerary expenditure and ceremonialism receive heightened customary expression; but beneath their apparent consolidation of the existing status categories these men introduce new ones. We can now ask what roles enterprising farmers must play at a level wider than that of homestead politics, and what role-conflicts are produced and reconciled in their doing so.

The switch to marketing copra rather than palm wine has moved the Giriama from involvement in a local economy, confined to Mijikenda, to one determined by international market factors. Enterprising farmers and traders have invested more than anyone else in the switch. They are obliged to heed, or to attempt personally to influence, political decisions which affect their enterprises, but which are made on their behalf by such agents of the central government as administrative, agricultural, and co-operative officers, the magistrate, and the local authorities. The most important decisions concern the allocation of development loans, changes in marketing and business legislation, and proposals for land-and-tree registration and consolidation. The latter have been proposed for some Mijikenda areas, though not yet Kaloleni, but Giriama farmers are fully aware that land-and-tree registration is imminent, as it is throughout Kenya's agricultural areas.

Issues of this kind inevitably demonstrate more clearly than ever that ultimate power lies with the central government and the local authorities. They also point up the enterprising farmer's dilemma. At the level of homestead politics he must subscribe to the common language of custom for a ready and reliable supply of information, witnesses, and property sellers. Yet he must also invest and participate in the decision-making bodies of the state as far as possible, which means subscribing, at least ostensibly, to the "progressive" and "anti-conservative" exhortations of these bodies. Locally he must be seen to defend custom, while at the national level he must be seen to transcend it.

In this chapter, therefore, I present three cases of men who can be regarded as being at different stages of solving this dilemma. They can be regarded also as having climbed to different levels of an entrepreneurial ladder: low, middle, and high. By focusing on each of them, I follow the interplay between local and wider forces in the incipient economic and political cleavage. Let me begin where the ladder is firmly rooted, at the level of homestead politics, for which the main public forum is the funeral ceremony.

The Peoples' Government

In the last chapter I showed that the funeral ceremony is the main, sanctioned, public occasion for accumulators to defer to elders, and it is the occasion, also, for them to assess their usefulness as witnesses, informers, or sellers of property. Returning to the middle-aged dance leader mentioned in Chapter 7, we can take him as an illustration of an accumulator whose assets of palms have increased over the past twenty years through a number of small purchases, but who still needs the support of witnesses and who continues to be on the look-out for further purchases. Preserving our metaphor, we may say that he is easing himself onto the first rung of the ladder.

Charo has made seven acquisitions, first of land alone and later of palms and land, between 1947, when he was a new, young homestead head, and 1966. In 1947 Charo's father died, and Charo left his job as a cook in town. He and his next youngest brother amicably divided their inheritance and kept some in trust for two other very young brothers. Together they bought some open land for the price of four heifers, with the intention of planting palms on it which they could tap for wine to sell. With the same aim Charo bought two more pieces of land in 1947 and in 1950, for 40 and 180 shillings, respectively, but this time without his brother.

Charo's first purchase of palms for producing copra was in 1958. He took four palms for 40 shillings, but not the land they stood on. From 1962 to 1966 he made three further and much larger acquisitions of both land and palms for 1,160, 610, and 500 shillings.

In each transaction Charo has had three or four main witnesses. No more than two witnesses in any one transaction have been brothers or other agnates. One or two witnesses in each transaction have been unrelated or only distantly related matrilaterially. All, however, can trace links to Charo through affinal serial linking and sometimes through direct affinity. Of these, only three elders have witnessed more than one transaction, one of them an octogenarian who witnessed three. A few years before the octogenarian's death in 1967, Charo had also called in the old man's only son as a witness. This son is now in the position to follow in his father's role as witness for Charo. Charo meanwhile continues to summon the help of the two other "regular" elders. There are also a couple of other elders whom he can call upon a second time when needed.

The main witnesses are related to Charo in various ways, but two general rules regarding recruitment are illustrated here. First, an agnate is said to be needed as a witness in any transaction so that there may be a spokesman for the property when it is inherited. This expectation is also held by the government court. To have the same agnate regularly witnessing a man's transactions is, however, considered unwise: he or a son might be chosen by the deceased's widows to inherit them and, as both agnatic spokesman and trustee for so much of a dead man's property, would be in a strong position to appropriate some of it. Second, it is therefore said to be better to have non-agnates as regular witnesses. Even then, some switching is desirable and, when the witness has conflicting loyalties to both buyer and seller, is also necessary. Sons of old witnesses may be invited so that as mature men they may carry on when their fathers die.

Charo is not high on the entrepreneurial ladder. He is definitely an accumulator but has made small purchases which amount now to a reasonable, but by no means indissoluble, family estate. He is investing in his three eldest sons' education, but has three wives and eight children and will need to expand his holdings well beyond their present size if the family estate is to remain economically viable after division when he dies. He must continue to emphasize the common language of custom. At a recent funeral, when eating meat in the company of elders, he stated that he would retire as dance leader because of his age. But his fellow elders on the clan council asked him to stay on to "control the younger members" a request which he accepted despite his complaint that organizing the dances as well as working on the council took valuable time from his farming.

The most recent and most valuable of Charo's acquisitions were in 1962, 1965, and 1966. For each of these Charo asked a literate man in the neighbourhood to write down the details on the page of an ordinary note pad. None of the parties to the transaction could write his signature, but the text took the form of first-person declarations of sale: "I, *X* son of *Y* have sold my land and palms to . . .". Charo carries these documents on his person. The 1962 sale was actually witnessed in the Kaloleni chief's office with the chief's clerk as scribe. Charo's witnesses had not objected at the time, but at a neighbourhood funeral ceremony shortly afterward Charo was pointedly asked by other elders why he had needed to use the chief's office. Did he not trust the people's government? Thereafter he did not ask his witnesses to the chief's compound. What is this people's government which Charo is expected to respect, and how does it conflict with the use of formal government machinery?

A notion of their own traditional government is, almost by definition, a feature of all ethnic groups incorporated first in colonies and later in independent states (R. Cohen and J. Middleton 1970, pp.24–30). The Giriama and other Mijikenda groups may have had government in the nineteenth century which fell half-way between centralised and uncentralised political systems, but this is difficult to substantiate. What is relevant for contemporary politics is that in each of the nine Mijikenda groups, the tradition of maintaining a ruling "capital" has persisted. In fact, this capital *(kaya)* is no more than a symbol. It consists of a site surrounded by bush into which only a few elders and their wives or persons with special permission from the *kaya* elders may go. The leading elders of ordinary homestead neighbourhoods like Tsakani and the elders of the Mijikenda Union claim that the *kaya* elders are of an age-group *(rika)* senior to themselves and that they are a repository of customary law and ritual. They emphasise the gerontocratic principle to legitimate their own influence.

During the development of nationalist politics in the Kenya coastal area in the 1950s, elders in the Mijikenda Union used their own and the *kaya* elders' legitimacy to speak and act on behalf of the Mijikenda people in order to mobilise support at the local homestead level for the younger, urban-based politicians operating on an all-Kenya front against the British colonial government. In order to advertise the extent of their influence they focused on local issues, including boundary disputes, opposition to proposals for land registration and consolidation, the reconstruction of *kaya* sites, and the defence of land around existing *kaya* sites.[1] I cannot present further details here, but it is clear from the issues mentioned that the organised influence of elders rested on local matters which related to developments in the use of land for palm growing.

Even since independence, these elders, or those who have succeeded them, have seen fit to defend their people's government. Now, however, the threat is not a colonial government but a judiciary run by younger, more educated men and a local administration more positively bent on rapid economic development than was the preceding colonial one. Enterprising farmers receive more encouragement and, most important, can acquire official recognition in this new era, as, in an instance already mentioned, Charo made use of the chief's scribe to witness a transaction. Other enterprising farmers sometimes use the district officer and even the chief in this way. It is believed, quite reasonably, that any man who has one of these among his witnesses would be well equipped to defend his rights in a government court if contested. But this development threatens the mediatory role of elders. The enterprising farmer is thus confronted with an acute dilemma of how to strike a balance between maintaining local goodwill and support and yet making use of the greater legal protection offered by the government administration.

The Central Government

Accumulators like Charo, who are still climbing the lower rungs of the entrepreneurial ladder, will continue to observe the common language of custom by concurring with elders' requests. True entrepreneurs, however, have diversified their economic assets and capital. They have lessened their financial dependence on copra and may own a shop or two, perhaps a tractor and plough, or even a transport truck or bus. The more men diversify, the more they are likely to contest and modify the existing language of custom. Investment in palms continues, however, to be economically useful, and so such men continue to use funeral ceremonies for recruiting support and gauging the progress of rivals. But they may also turn to the local government administration for such additional external support as loans, which will not incur elders' disapproval, and legal protection, which will. It is no coincidence that the most economically secure entrepreneurs in Kaloleni location have in recent years requested that their wills be drawn up with the help of the district administration and government judiciary, who encourage such innovations.

A locally famous court case which occurred in 1966 at Kaloleni court signalled a new power for enterprising men, namely the power of state protection. The case concerns the third most wealthy Giriama in the country and so represents an extreme example. I give it as an illustration of what changes in customary law may be introduced at the top rung of the entrepreneurial ladder.

In the case (Civil Case No.110/66 Kaloleni Government Court), a young man succeeded in convincing the court that, through his own entrepreneurial skills, he had earned exclusive rights of ownership over a shop, a cafe, and a transport business, for which the original capital had been inherited in 1960 by an older and senior half-brother who had been a full brother of the deceased, but who had left the running of the business to the younger man. The significant facts of the case, in which the older half-brother was plaintiff, were: that the clan elders had appointed him as heir to the original business, but that his younger half-brother had actually worked on the business and expanded it; that after the appointment of an heir this younger half-brother had, without the knowledge and consent of the senior man, sought advice and help from the district officer and the government public trustee (a measure which later enabled the younger man to prove that he alone had settled the debts of the original business and had expanded it); and that, in defiance of customary expectations and the demands of the clan elders who had sanctioned the inheritance, the young man had refused to co-habit with two widows of the deceased half-brother, on the grounds of being a Christian monogamist.

Between Two Governments

Most entrepreneurs in Kaloleni stand half-way between an accumulator like Charo, who is still wholly dependent on palms, and the wealthy businessman just mentioned, whose dependence on them is now fractional. Typical are the three entrepreneurs of Tsakani, two of whom became therapeutic Muslims. One of these two is well on the way to the upper echelons. He owns two small shops and has purchased a tractor and plough on loan, but still depends heavily on the sale of copra to subsidise his other enterprises. The second grows and stores maize, which he farms on a large scale and which he sells during times of scarcity. His activities are smaller in scale, produce less profit, and are at present much less diverse. He is even more dependent on a subsidy from copra production. His career illustrates well not only the pressures of elders, to which an increasingly successful farmer is subject, but it illustrates also the change in power relations in the past few years which have favoured the emergence of entrepreneurs, but which have brought organisations of elders' like the Mijikenda Union into a direct confrontation with the independent government's local administration and judiciary. I briefly describe his career and some of these accompanying developments and then discuss their sociological significance.

Kirao's father died in 1955. As eldest brother he returned from his semi-skilled job in Kwale district to become head of the homestead. He had saved a little money from his job and was able to sponsor modest but acceptable first and second funerals for his father. For this act of filial piety, he earned the warm approval of the elders. His father had come to Tsakani in 1938 and had bought 15 acres of land from a man of Mwaparwa clan for a bull and a cow. The land had a few palms, but was mostly virgin soil. Kirao and his two brothers were appointed heirs under Kirao's headship.

In 1958 Kirao used the bridewealth received at the marriage of a sister to buy for 1,100 shillings an unspecified number of palms and a plot of land from a nearby homestead head. He promised a younger brother, who would normally have used the bridewealth for his own marriage, that within three years the investment would have brought sufficient income to recoup the cash and provide the brother with bridewealth. With income from the sale of coconuts and copra from his new purchase, Kirao was able to turn to good use the 15 acres of virgin land inherited from his father. He used it to grow maize which he sold to the surrounding homesteads. He eventually sought advice from the agricultural department, which gave him a small loan to buy special maize seed and fertilizer. He had constructed a makeshift granary in which he stored the grain, which he then sold only during the lean months of the following year when ordinary farmers' stocks were low. Four years later he had saved enough to fulfil his promise to his younger brother, only a year late.

But Kirao's superb economic management and success brought its own problems. It is said that people wondered at his success. How did his maize survive while that of others succumbed to drought? It was rumoured at one stage that, though he was a young man, he must have had the power to practise sorcery. On one celebrated occasion in the early sixties, three elders of Tsakani asked him to "help" them with a few of his maize seeds. Kirao explained that they were expensive and could only be bought from the agricultural department, and that he had limited supplies. This made the elders angry, and one even threatened to use sorcery to make sure his maize would die.

It was at this point, during a period of undoubted unpopularity and stress, that Kirao became possessed by an Islamic spirit which obliged him to become a therapeutic Muslim. From all accounts, it does seem that he genuinely became very thin and looked ill. Even those who had resented his "meanness" expressed concern. He did, after all, sell them maize at a price below that of the packeted maize flour available from the shops.

For a while, it seems, public criticism of him faded. Thereafter, however, he was attacked on more substantial issues, two of which reached the government court and the chief's office. He successfully counter-attacked on both issues, which I shall describe in chronological order.

Showdown 1.   *Kirao versus the elders of Tsakani*

In 1964 four elders of Tsakani approached Kirao with the claim that the 15 acres of land bought by his father belonged to Kirao's patrilateral parallel cousin. They claimed that it was not Kirao's father, but this elder cousin's father, who had paid the cow and bull to the original owner. Two of the elders who made this protest were committee members of the Mijikenda Union. One is now deceased, and the other is one of Tsakani's three neighbourhood doctors. When Kirao refused to accept their claim, he was greatly scolded by the elders who asked him how "as a child" he could possibly know the nature of the transaction. This initial encounter ended when Kirao declared that he would take the matter to the government court. From independent discussion with both parties to the dispute, the Mijikenda Union elder who is a neighbourhood doctor is said to have exclaimed something like, "Why do you have to do this [take the matter to the government court]? Why can't you allow us to settle the matter in our [traditional] Giriama way?". Nevertheless, Kirao refused to have the matter settled either by neighbourhood moot or through the auspices of the Mijikenda Union. He insisted on having them go straight to court, won the case, and then asked the agricultural officer to survey his boundaries. The request was granted. The cousin, in whose name the case had been brought, had to pay 300 shillings in costs (some of them, the expenses of visiting the land and interrogating witnesses in neighbouring homesteads). One of Kirao's chief witnesses was a paternal uncle of his father and also one of Kaloleni's most famous doctors. Another important witness was an unrelated elder, who was also a neighbourhood doctor and who had originally been introduced to the practice by the doctor.

Showdown 2. The State Versus the People's Government

The second issue arose in 1967. On this occasion, the Mijikenda Union was represented principally by another committee member who lived in Tsakani and who was also a neighbourhood doctor. As the only literate committee member of the union branch, he drew up in Giriama the following charge against Kirao: "As secretary of the Mijikenda Union, I ask you, *X*, to give Shs.50/- *malu* [adultery compensation] to *Y* for adultery with his wife. His wife has admitted that you are her friend. Please do not fail to give the compensation or you will be accused".

The wife had confessed rather than take the oath of the (burning) axe *(kiraho cha tsoka)*. Kirao protested that this oath was false and anyway was illegal in the government's eyes. He pointed out that the chief (who was appointed by the government) might give a permit for adjudication by a different and, in the government's view, less harmful vegetable or fruit oath *(kiraho cha tserembe* or *kapapayu)*. He would agree to take this oath himself. As an act of good faith, he himself deposited 50 shillings with the chief. The chief did not, in the end, allow the oath to be given (though permission is sometimes given—a practice dating from colonial times). Instead, therefore, Kirao gave the letter he had received from the Mijikenda Union to the young government court magistrate, who had himself opposed the recent increase in the union's influence in settling disputes. It was agreed that the letter should be used as evidence of interference and of the use of threats by the Mijikenda Union in the government court's activities. However, the secretary of the union had himself sent a copy of the letter to the chief and thus could legitimately claim to have acted openly. The situation was further complicated by the fact that the sub-chief for the area of which Tsakani is a part had assumed, like the chief, that the Mijikenda Union had the *de facto* authority to try the minor matter of an adultery charge. This has certainly been the case since the Mijikenda Union was recognised by the colonial government in 1945. Indeed, in the past it has been positively encouraged to shortcut judicial matters and save their having to come to court. The original demand for adultery compensation against Kirao was dropped because, by now, the issue was no longer between him and the Mijikenda Union elders.

The Result

The complicated situation was now as follows: the magistrate had for months expressed concern at the increased influence of the Mijikenda Union and appeared to see this issue as an occasion for curbing the union's activities by appealing to the district officer, the only non-Giriama and non-coastal person involved, and also the greatest authority. However, at this point the chief and sub-chief found themselves to be unwitting defenders of the Mijikenda Union. The union, in company with neighbourhood moots, had always been given a *de facto* right to settle disputes concerned with anything other than homicide, bodily injury, and severe cases of theft (though they might deal even with the latter two). The chief and sub-chief had dealt with the union on this assumption in this as they had in other cases. Now the chief was being asked by the district officer to state whether he considered that the Union had abused the trust given it. The chief had himself faced opposition which had been organised partly by the union over his method of local tax assessment and similar matters, and there was open conflict between him and the union. Not surprisingly, he sided with the young magistrate. The district officer ordered the union's judicial activities curtailed, and directed it in future to be "less political and more a welfare society as it was originally intended". (*Kilifi District Annual Report*, 1966.)

Kirao was severely criticised not only by the rebuked Union committee, but also by other elders, even some who had been personal rivals of members of the committee or who had been excluded from it. Elders as a body seemed to recognise that even their limited gerontocracy was on the wane. It is significant that Kirao had taken his stand at a time at which his enterprise was becoming securely based. He had shortly beforehand purchased 18 acres of almost entirely open land for 3,000 shillings. A few months afterward, however, he held a festival to honour a deceased classificatory paternal grandmother who had died in 1957, allegedly without a second funeral. This festival was a very lavish ceremony, heavily sponsored by Kirao. For the first time in months, Kirao was congratulated by elders for his generosity. He would move from one small group of elders to another, talking, but, as a therapeutic Muslim, neither drinking nor eating with them. He was beginning again the task of finding witnesses, informers, and potential sellers of property through the common, if modified, language of custom.

Analysis of Kirao's Case

For the sake of simplicity, we can contrast two policies of local government administration regarding the application of Mijikenda customary law. The first is the essentially *laissez-faire* judicial policy of the colonial administration. The second is a policy more positively directed at centralising judicial authority in the local administration. The first characterises much of the colonial era. Even in 1947 there was an attempt to strengthen the power of the traditional institutions run by elders, in which the Mijikenda Union and neighbourhood moots were given considerable autonomy. The second policy was most obviously put into practice after independence in December 1963. Magistrates were expected to be better educated than their predecessors and tended therefore to be younger. This parallels the intention of many independent African states to destroy the "conservatism" inherent in the chiefships and court systems which were established and continued during colonial times.

In his first showdown with the elders, Kirao wisely recruited two doctors—one, an important one. He fought the battle in the idiom of his opponents. This is an idiom going back to the *laissez-faire* judicial policy of colonial times: the elders of neighbourhood moots and the Mijikenda Union require ritual sanctions, including the use of oaths, as tools of their profession, and many of them are themselves neighbourhood doctors. With the emergence of the second administrative policy aimed at destroying conservatism, Kirao was able to challenge the elders and the Mijikenda Union, but he only did so when he had reached a degree of economic security. Even then, he returned after his victory to offer the elders customary gifts of appeasement.

The Entrepreneurial Ladder. Comparative Analysis of the three cases of: (1) Charo, the accumulator; (2) Kirao, the entrepreneurial farmer; and (3) the wealthy Giriama businessman

1. Charo stands lowest on the entrepreneurial ladder and so shows himself to be subject to the strongest sanctions of elders to observe the common language of custom. He must eat and drink with them and sit as a junior member on their councils. He is not yet a sufficiently prominent farmer to be given a development loan by the agricultural department or to have strong allies in the government administration. He is one of many accumulators, who number ten of Tsakani's thirty economic managers.

2. Kirao has reached a level of success which enables him to call upon the supreme power of the state in the form of the local government administration during times of crisis. He is also wealthy enough to repair a breach in his dialogue of custom and conscience with the elders. But before reaching this level he underwent a critical stage in which he introduced agricultural innovations and had to appear to be blatantly ungenerous by refusing to hand out special maize seeds he had purchased from the agricultural department. It was at this point that an Islamic spirit possessed him and enabled him to control the social distance between himself and the elders.

3. The wealthy Giriama businessman took a much more defiant stand against the demands of custom, the local effect of which appeared to be commensurate with his economic importance. He did not undergo conversion to Islam, but, probably because he had received a few year's education at the mission school, became a nominal Christian and used the Christian demand for monogamy as a partial weapon in his stand against custom. He is one of only five or so entrepreneurs in Kaloleni who have minimised their direct dependence on agriculture and whose enterprises now mostly consist of shops, trucks, and buses. The sign of things to come is evidenced in the recent (1966/1967) attempt by some of these businessmen to move into important positions in the Kilifi county council either as councillors or as members of special committees concerned with economic development and co-operatives in the area. But this is another story, which has yet to unfold.

Conclusions

In the last chapter I portrayed the funeral ceremony as an important common occasion which enables young, enterprising farmers and older witnesses to assess their complementary needs with regard to each other. The ceremony has been described also as an arena in which rival competitors for palms may assess each other's social standing and prestige. At one level the funeral, by drawing together people who are variously related to each other, expresses wide-scale acceptance of a common language of custom. Yet, at another level it facilitates the creation of wealth differences, with palms being increasingly concentrated in the hands of a minority of enterprising farmers. It does this by stressing lavish expenditure, which, like bridewealth transactions, saps the resources of many men, causing them to sell their palms and land to an enterprising few.

The funeral ceremony may well be regarded as the central forum of the local gerontocracy. But, as I have shown in this chapter, the wider encapsulating political system has begun to nibble at this gerontocracy since Kenya's political independence. There has developed a policy more positively directed at encouraging African economic development, including entrepreneurship.[2] By using the image of an entrepreneurial ladder, we find, not surprisingly, that those at the bottom of the ladder must continue to subscribe to the customary demands of elders: they are insiders in the community and can only succeed in buying and defending palms by nurturing ties with elders who may act as supporters.

As men move up the ladder, they need to diversify and reduce their economic dependence on palms. Diversification may take the form of growing and selling crops other than palms. The example used here was of a man who cornered the local market in maize. But cashew nuts, cassava, and citrus fruits provide other openings. Nevertheless, the farmer who has diversified in this way still remains a farmer. As such, he continues to depend on good contacts with his neighbours for information about land for sale. In a society in which government registration of land has not been introduced and in which an enterprising farmer's land is likely to be fragmented because of his making separate purchases over the years, he also continues to need the support of respected elders as witnesses to his claims.

There is an ambivalence in the status of the enterprising farmer: he must remain an insider in the local community in order to acquire the necessary contacts for success; yet he must innovate (for example, by using special seeds, fertilizer, and timed planting schedules, and by crop rotation, as well as by using a mechanical plough) and may therefore be accused by elders of upsetting the *status quo*. I suggest that among some enterprising farmers conversion to what I have called therapeutic Islam corresponds with this ambivalent status: it saves the enterprising farmer from overfrequent and overinvolved commensal relations and yet allows him to continue to subscribe to customary spheres of activity, including marriage and funeral ceremonies, which benefit him in the long term.

This status complements the ambivalent role of elder, which, as I have shown in previous chapters, paradoxically sanctions in its performance the redistributional economic ideal and the more dominant accumulative one. My concern in the next chapter is with the theoretical implications of the ritualization of such ambivalent roles, statuses, and situations.

Standing at the top of the entrepreneurial ladder in a relatively unambivalent relationship to the elders are the few wealthy Giriama traders in Kaloleni. They have diversified to the extent of relying primarily on non-farming enterprises and demands. They work mainly within the framework of the local government administration. Their sources of support are fellow members of this wider elite, who will surely in time bring about government land-and-tree registration and consolidation. It can be speculated, however, that if, as seems likely, they also move into positions of regional, and even national, political importance, they will then again need local support, in the form, perhaps, of votes. In many other parts of Kenya which have experienced earlier African economic development, this process is already under way. In such a situation we may expect the language of custom to be modified further, but to retain geographical distinctiveness.

These wealthy Giriama traders constitute a boundary placed round this study. I have been more concerned with the interpersonal changes occurring among farmers as external economic opportunities and the monetization of all transactions have diffused the capitalist spirit. I turn now to suggesting the place of this study in anthropological theory.

NOTES

1. Much could be written on the activities of elders who at various times have worked through the Mijikenda Union. Information on the union from documentary sources is slender, and the best is still available from the elders, themselves. But I mention the following references, most of them drawn to my attention by Mr. R.F. Morton: *Digo District Annual Report*, 1945, 1946, 1948–1952, and 1954; *Kilifi District Annual Report*, 1953; *Malindi Sub-district Annual Report*, 1948 and 1949; *Coast Province Annual Report*, 1945, 1947 1949, and 1952; *Kilifi District Handing Over Reports*, 19/3/46, 4/3/49, and 14/4/49.

2. The contrasting policies, in this respect, of neighbouring Tanzania suggest the possibility of an interesting complementary study.

9. Conclusions

I have described a process of ecological change among a small group of farmers which has had radical technological, political, and economic consequences for them. The switch from an internal economy based on palm wine to an external one based on copra has involved a switch from a re-distributional to an accumulative, or capitalist, mode of exchange relations. Stated thus, the study reveals little that is new. But I have focused the analysis on what may be called the "mystifying" properties of custom and ritual under conditions of change.

What do I mean here by mystification? I refer to the discrepancy, sometimes the outright contradiction, between the publicly manifest cultural justification for a role or activity (how people justify their belief in the purpose of the role or activity) and the long-term, hidden or latent consequences for the society of this role or activity. Not all culturally valued roles and activities have this built-in ambivalence of short-term expression and long-term effect, but those that do are worthy of sociological explanation.

We have some familiar, though varied, examples of such activities: Gluckman (1960) demonstrated how the "licence in ritual" can actually reassert the social order by seeming in the short term to flout the *status quo;* Leach (1954, p. 278) pointed out that ritual may be seen not simply as a "mechanism of integration" but also as one of disintegration. From this we can argue that ritual is *always* likely to convey both harmony and disharmony, according to the social positions of its participants: to those in power its message is that of solidarity, while to those who are planning to usurp this power the ritual offers itself as a long-term weapon with which to establish their independence or dominance. This is an example of how the communicative (symbolic) ambivalence of ritual activity facilitates social change.

Radical change of the kind described in this book is common in much of the Third World. It is by no means the only kind of radical change; other examples can be found in the past and contemporary history of industrialized nations, as well. In many situations involving the substitution of an accumulative for a re-distributional or other mode of exchange, there is a discrepancy between what is publicly proclaimed to be the existing authority system and the new, more powerful but less "legitimate" sources of influence.

Weber's documentation of the relationship between religious ascetism, parsimony, and capitalist success in the Industrial Revolution was not specifically concerned with the problem of religious or symbolic mystification. But it is reasonable to suggest that an important property of the Protestant ethic was its capacity to sanction the ideal of a constant equality of opportunity for all, while at the same time supporting the political principle that power went increasingly to those who most capitalized on accumulated assets. Thus, we are told that Calvinist leaders opposed the "politically privileged commercial, putting-out, and colonial capitalism" under the Stuarts. Instead, over and against this "they placed the individualistic motives of rational legal acquisition by virtue of one's own ability and initiative" (Weber 1930, p. 179). Coupled with the ideal of parsimony, this was bound to lead to large-scale saving, as a legitimate fruit of labour, and from there to the productive investment of capital by a minority.

We are dealing here with the problem of the mystification of social inequality (Cohen 1969b, pp. 220–221). We can ask what kinds of custom, role, or ideology are most suited to the task of smuggling in, beneath their manifest prescription, new roles and new values commensurate with these roles. On the basis of Weber's analysis, we can suggest that the ascetic ideal, including the deliberate restriction on the enjoyment and consumption of possessions and luxuries, is a suitable prescription, first, for private saving, then for capital accumulation, then for productive investment, and finally for rampant capitalism and the beginnings of mass production, which in the end contradicts the ascetic ideal. Asceticism, in other words, has this built-in ambiguity of short-term expression and long-term effect under the conditions of an expanding economy.

Asceticism would not be a suitable prescription for entrepreneurial success in the still relatively undifferentiated economic circumstances of Giriama society. Men are regarded there as equal, and those who wish to rise above the rest have to emphasise not asceticism but customary generosity. They have to balance successfully the cost of generosity against the property gains acquired through their contacts. If and when there is a firmly established minority of Giriama entrepreneurs who have diversified beyond reliance on farming, then we may expect the ascetic ideal (as followed in Kenya, for instance, by Kikuyu business-men; see Marris and Somerset 1971, pp. 83–90) to be diffused as a further stage in the development of the capitalist spirit. Whatever the stage, an important sociological task is to understand how these transformations of ideology are accommodated within existing fields of custom, belief, and ritual.

In Giriama I can identify three such fields. Each proclaims an ideal which supports the re-distributional economy and the gerontocracy. Yet, under the protection, so to speak, of this ideal, a new, more fundamental but initially illicit capitalistic principle is smuggled in. I call these types of mystification, paradoxes of custom.

First, among the Giriama of Kaloleni there is the overarching idiom of an intergenerational cleavage. All cultures have some expression of generational differences, but these may vary considerably in their usefulness as paradoxes of custom. Why were they used as such among the Kaloleni Giriama? It is tempting to look immediately to the apparent existence in the nineteenth century of an age-set organization among Giriama and suggest that this once-important cultural phenomenon was revived under modern conditions. But there is little evidence for this. All one has are piecemeal but very important semantic and symbolic facets. Thus, *rika* (pl. *marika*) remains an important term denoting general grades of age, as does *mutumia* (an elder), while the traditional capital *(kaya)* is even nowadays inhabited only by a few very old men and old women, who are supposed to be of an even higher age grade than the average *mutumia*. Similarly, the Giriama include among a number of personal naming systems an important one which designates adults according to their children's or grandchildren's names. As H. and C. Geertz (1964) demonstrate, this practice of teknonymy helps to distinguish the main generational strata. There is little doubt that these and other cultural facets lend themselves well to a marked intergenerational expression of many relations.

However, the general notion that age, seniority, and authority go together is common also to many African farming communities which lack such persisting cultural features. Its emphasis among Giriama can be put down to contemporary and recent facts. Let me consider briefly the restricted economic and subsistence system as it existed in Kaloleni in the 1920s and early 1930s.

Half a century ago Giriama exported reasonable quantities of grain. But from about 1914, possibly as a result of their defeat in the rising against the British, their exports dwindled till they entered an economic recession. Those Giriama who migrated to Kaloleni and those already there acquired a new economic lease on life when they concentrated on palms. They produced wine for themselves and for a limited number of other Mijikenda areas. However, it was still not until they exported copra and coconuts on a large scale through the Asian middlemen in Kaloleni that there were opportunities for individuals to accumulate large holdings of palms and land.

Up to this point, and in the absence of significant migration of labour for cash, the economy was essentially an internal, re-distributional one. As now, sons had little alternative to depending on fathers, paternal uncles, or elder brothers for bridewealth and inheritance. But unlike now, even where there were young homestead heads, the re-distributional economy limited the development of the inverse correlation of economic success and age which is so apparent today. In other words, a gerontocracy constituted probably the most suitable loose form of political and judicial organization, under the circumstances. For the colonial administration in an allegedly backward area, it also probably constituted the easiest method of indirect rule below the government-appointed chief.

The opportunities for capital accumulation and productive investment through palms in an internationally controlled economy are relatively recent. A minority of younger men, all still under fifty, have taken advantage of them by acquiring property, mostly from older family heads. Small wonder, then, that intergenerational differences, already entrenched in custom and ritual, should be used as a cover for a growing economic cleavage between accumulators and losers of property. In other words, conflicts between accumulators and losers are frequently fought as issues between elders and juniors; custom is seen to be done, yet is thereby threatened by more fundamentally divisive forces.

The second paradox of custom is central to all three and concerns the actual role of elders. As elders they are preferred as witnesses by the government court and local moots. Much of their status as witnesses, and thereby the local gerontocracy, is supported by continued recognition of the value of agnation in inheritance, marriage, and settlement organization. Yet, as witnesses, they frequently attach themselves almost as clients to the young enterprising farmers, who have acquired most of their property not through agnatic entitlement but through purchase or mortgage. Both enterprising and ordinary farmers, but, by definition, especially the former, need witnesses because land and trees have not yet been registered or consolidated in Kaloleni, despite the post-war rush to acquire or lay claim to them. Through their activities as witnesses, then, elders uphold the gerontocratic ideal and yet subscribe to the capitalistic spirit which in the long term threatens to destroy the ideal that age is the prerequisite of authority.

The third paradox of custom follows from the second and concerns what Bohannan (1959), Barth (1966), and others have called exchange spheres, among which I focus on bridewealth and reciprocal funerary expenditure. Among the Giriama, bridewealth secures genetricial as well as uxorial rights in a woman, who must not be from her husband's clan. In the event of divorce, bridewealth is recoverable, but children are not. Bridewealth legitimizes successors to deceased agnates and heirs to their property and so is a corner-stone of the agnatic principle and therefore of the mediatory role of elders. But bridewealth payments are heavy, and they have become monetized and inflated as the economy has switched to copra production. They drain the resources of poorer men, causing them to sell palms and land to young, enterprising farmers, who have the resources to meet their own bridewealth expenditure. More than this, as an exchange system bridewealth entails the circulation of large sums of money, which can be used as capital for the purchase of more land and palms by enterprising farmers with existing alternative resources. As a modified, though certainly strengthened, customary exchange sphere, bridewealth transactions are seen to uphold the norms of agnation and the authority of elders, yet in the long term they facilitate the emergence of a cleavage between a minority of young property owners and the rest.

Similarly, reciprocal funeral expenditure has escalated in the same period. As well as marking off the ordinary from the enterprising farmers, it has become a kind of political stock-market for competing property accumulators. And yet, even there, a main idiom in which relations are conducted is that of an intergenerational division of privileges, with due deference accorded to elders.

These paradoxes of custom can be regarded as concessions (not necessarily consciously recognised as such) made by enterprising farmers who otherwise are gradually contesting the *status quo*. The need for witnesses, and potential sellers of property is thus a good, practical reason why it is inexpedient for enterprising farmers to disregard the common language of custom. It is unlikely that all, if any, of them think in quite these instrumental terms. Wherever ideals are pro-claimed, even in the face of facts, there is likely to be a common symbolizing process enabling people to recognize the ideals and to respond to them. Both enterprising and ordinary Giriama farmers, the young and the old—and indeed all Giriama men and women—share a common belief in sorcery and its effects and in the modes of divination and ritual cure used to counter those effects. All these constitute the symbols of what Turner has called a community of suffering (1957 p. xxi).

Only elders may be traditional doctors, and in this respect they hold a trump card. It is true that enterprising farmers may become Muslim through involun-tary possession by an Islamic spirit, which introduces a commensal and ritual line of demarcation between themselves, elders, and other people who are not Muslim, but they continue to make use of common curative symbols or, as Leach might put it, continue to operate a common language of ritual and custom. For this reason the pragmatically useful role of elders as witnesses is given mystical credibility.

By the same token, the paradoxes of custom are not seen to be such. Only their legitimate side is shown. The growing cleavage is hidden by common appeals to the gerontocratic and agnatic ideals which are so frequently ritualized. With reference to his and Turner's work, Professor Gluckman formulates the proposi-tion that "mystical beliefs and ritual practices are most significant where they 'cloak' fundamental discrepancies or *conflicts* between the principles on which a society is based, or between conflicting processes set at work in a society by an apparently definite single principle" (1965, p. 223–224; my italics). Just two examples of such conflict are that between the rules of matriliny and virilocality among the Ndembu of Zambia studied by Turner, and that between the beneficial role of the fruitful Zulu wife who strengthens her husband's lineage and the potentially divisive role she has as reference point for the fission of the same lineage according to the rules of the Zulu house-property complex. These and other examples occur in relatively unchanging social structures. If they are fol-lowed through time, as Turner has done, the change observed is of a repetitive or cyclical nature (Gluckman 1965, pp. 279–285).

Ndembu society, it is true, has seen the establishment of Pax Britannica, the introduction of cash-cropping and wage-labour, and the disappearance of hunting for game, which once symbolised male dominance. But throughout these changes there has been no apparent alteration of the basic structure of power and privilege. Turner himself suggests that we might see more fundamental change if we moved back historically to what may have been the origins of present-day Ndembu society. He says that it is likely that a settled society with matriliny and uxorilo-cality (which principles harmonise) was invaded by a politically superior one with patriliny and virilocality (which also harmonise). The mix that emerged was a society which preserved matriliny but adopted virilocality.

In a recent work Turner calls this a basic contradiction rather than simply a conflict of principles (1968, p. 279) and suggests that Ndembu may be "a transi-tional social type"—that is, morphologically half-way between a matrilinealuxorilocal society and a patrilineal-virilocal one. This is no more than intelligent speculation and would require the evidence of oral history. But, if true, it means that, with the limited time-span that his data allowed him, Turner was in fact analysing a small phase of a longer-term development. What in the short term appear in his study as conflicting principles reconcilable through ritual mechanisms of redress, may in the longer term be contradictory principles, one of which is emerging dominant while the other is atrophying.

If Ndembu *is* a "transitional social type", is it moving more toward virilocality and from there to patriliny also, or more toward matriliny and from there to uxorilocality? As well as a possible "modern" development to bilateral inheritance and succession and to neolocality, either of these seems possible (Watson 1958 and Douglas 1969). This, too, is speculative. But it does suggest that Bailey's well known distinction (1957a; 1960, p. 7) between institutional conflict which does not alter the basic structure of power and privilege, and institutional contradiction which does precipitate radical change, is thus of crucial importance in studying the mystification of emerging social inequality. Among the Giriama of Kaloleni considerable ecological and economic change has occurred within a short period. I have therefore been able to observe situations in which custom, sanctified through mystical belief and practice, in the short term cloaks fundamental contradictions set up in the society, but in the long term facilitates radical change by admitting, so to speak, new sources of economic and political power.

The Giriama have had their periods of economic expansion in the past, and it is quite likely that at those times paradoxes of custom similar to or other than the three discussed here facilitated radical change while giving short-term support to an accepted ideal. It does seem reasonable to suggest, however, that never before have Giriama become so dependent on the forces of an international market of supply and demand.

If we accept that the once considerable economic self-sufficiency of the Giriama is now irretrievable, then we can accept that, coupled with the official encouragement given to it by the Kenya government, the capitalist spirit is in the process of limiting the effectiveness of the local gerontocracy: even without land registration, enterprising farmers may increasingly turn for legal testimony and protection to lawyers or government agents, rather than to the elders.

This is not to suggest that under future conditions of radical change there may not be further paradoxes of custom among the Giriama. Wherever there is radical change, there are likely to be hidden contradictions between the public justification of activities sanctioned by a customary ideal and their long-term consequences. This continues to be a fruitful field of research for anthropologists in both contemporary industrial and agricultural societies. For, insofar as we follow unquestioningly many customs and conventions in our own particular cultures, we are all mystified into accepting certain assumptions about our place in society and about human existence generally. Yet at the same time we remain unaware of the long-term implications of our values and beliefs.

Bibliography

Bailey, F. G. 1957. "Political Change in the Kondmals." *Eastern Anthropologist* 11: 88–106.

———. 1957. *Caste and the Economic Frontier.* Manchester University Press.

———. 1960. *Caste, Tribe and Nation.* Manchester University Press.

———. 1969. *Strategems and Spoils.* Oxford: Blackwell.

Barnes, J. A. 1967. "The Frequency of Divorce." In Epstein, A. L., ed., pp. 47–100.

Barth, F. 1959. *Political Leadership Among Swat Pathans.* London School of Economics Social Anthropology Monograph 19. London: Athlone Press.

———. 1963. *The Role of the Entrepreneur in Social Change in Northern Norway.* Bergen: Norwegian University Press.

———. 1967. "Exchange Spheres in Dafur." In *Themes in Economic Anthropology*, ed. R. Firth. Association of Social Anthropologists Monograph 6. London: Tavistock.

Beidelman, T.O. 1966. "The Ox and Nuer Sacrifice". *Man* (N.S.) 1: 453–467.

Belshaw, C. S. 1965. *Traditional Exchange and Modern Markets.* Englewood Cliffs, N.J.: Prentice-Hall.

Bohannan, P. 1959. "The Impact of Money on an African Subsistence Economy." *The Journal of Economic History* 19/4: 491–503.

Brokensha, D. 1966. *Social Change at Larteh, Ghana.* Oxford: Clarendon Press.

Caplan, L. 1970. *Land and Social Change in East Nepal.* Berkeley and Los Angeles: University of California Press.

Caplan, P. 1969. "Cognatic Descent Groups on Mafia Island, Tanzania." *Man* (N.S.) 4: 419–431.

Cashmore, T.H.R. 1965. "Studies in District Administration in the East Africa Protectorate 1895–1918." Ph.D. dissertation, Cambridge University.

Champion, A. M. 1967. *The Agiryama of Kenya*, ed. J. Middleton. Occasional Paper 25. London: Royal Anthropological Institute.

Cohen, A. 1969a. *Custom and Politics in Urban Africa.* Berkeley and Los Angeles: University of California Press.

———. 1969b. "Political Anthropology: the Analysis of the Symbolism of Power Relations." *Man* (N.S.) 4: 215–235.

Cohen, R., and Middleton, J. 1970. *From Tribe to Nation.* Scranton: Chandler.

Cotran, E. 1968. *Restatement of African Law: Kenya. The Law of Marriage and Divorce*, ed. D. Allott, vol. 1. London: Sweet & Maxwell.

Dalton, G. 1954. "Traditional Production in Primitive African Economies." *Quarterly Journal of Economics* 76: 360–378. Reprinted in *Tribal and Peasant Economies*, ed. G. Dalton. 1967. New York: Natural History Press.

Douglas, M. 1969. "Is Matriliny Doomed in Africa?" In *Man in Africa*, eds. M. Douglas and P. Kaberry. London: Tavistock.

Elwin, V. 1955. *The Religion of an Indian Tribe*. Bombay: Cumberlege; Oxford University Press.

Epstein, A. L., ed. 1967. *The Craft of Social Anthropology*. London: Tavistock.

Epstein, T. S. 1968. *Capitalism: Primitive and Modern*. Manchester University Press.

Geertz, C. 1963. *Peddlers and Princes*. University of Chicago Press.

———, and H. 1964. "Teknonymy in Bali: Parenthood, Age-Grading and Genealogical Amnesia." *Journal of the Royal Anthropological Institute* 94: 94–108. Also in *Marriage, Family and Residence* eds. P. Bohannan and J. Middleton. 1968. New York: Natural History Press.

Gluckman, M. 1960. *Custom and Conflict in Africa*. Oxford: Blackwell.

———. 1965. *Politics, Law and Ritual in Tribal Society*. Oxford: Blackwell.

Goody, J. 1957. "Anomie in Ashanti?" *Africa* 27: 356–363.

Gulliver, P. H. 1963. *Social Control in an African Society*. London: Routledge.

———. 1971. *Neighbours and Networks*. Berkeley and Los Angeles: University of California Press.

Hill, P. 1970. *Studies in Rural Capitalism*. Cambridge University Press.

Hoebel, E. A. 1940. "The Political Organization and Law-Ways of the Comanche Indians." *American Anthropologist* vol. 42, no. 3, pt. 2 (supplement).

Kelly, W. F. P. 1960. *Kilifi District Gazeteer*. Nairobi: Kenya National Archives.

Kilifi District Political Records and Annual Reports. Nairobi: Kenya National Archives.

Leach, E. R. 1954. *Political Systems of Highland Burma*. Reprinted 1964. London: Bell.

Lewis, I. 1966. "Spirit Possession and Deprivation Cults." *Man* (N.S.) 1: 307–329.

Lloyd, P. 1962. *Yoruba Land Law*. London: Oxford University Press.

Long, N. 1968. *Social Change and the Individual*. Manchester University Press.

Mair, L. P. 1940. *Native Marriage in Buganda*. Memo 19. London: International African Institute.

Marris, P., and Somerset, A. 1971. *African Businessmen*. London: Routledge, for Institute of Community Studies.

Mayer, A. C. 1966. "The Significance of Quasi-Groups in the Study of Complex Societies." In *The Social Anthropology of Complex Societies*, ed. M. P. Banton. Association of Social Anthropologists Monograph 4. London: Tavistock.

Meggit, M. J. 1965. *The Lineage System of the Mae-Enga of New Guinea*. London: Oliver and Boyd.

Merton, R. K. 1957. *Social Theory and Social Structure*. New York: The Free Press.

Mitchell, J. C. 1967. "On Quantification in Social Anthropology." In A. L. Epstein, ed. 1967.

Ngala, R. G. 1949. *Nchi na Desturi za Wagiriama*. Nairobi: The Eagle Press.

Nicholas, R. W. 1965. "Factions: A Comparative Analysis." In *Political Systems and the Distribution of Power*. Association of Social Anthropologists Monograph 2. London: Tavistock.

Parkin, D. J. 1968. "Medicines and Men of Influence." *Man* (N.S.) 3: 424–439.

———. 1970. "Politics of Ritual Syncretism." *Africa* 40: 1.

Pitt, D. 1970. *Tradition and Economic Progress in Samoa*. Oxford: Clarendon.

Prins, A. H. J. *The Coastal Tribes of the North-Eastern Bantu*. London: International African Institute.

Southall, A. W. c.1954. *Alur Society*. Cambridge: Heffer.

Spencer, P. 1965. *The Samburu: A Study of Gerontocracy in a Nomadic Tribe*. London: Routledge.

Taylor, D. R. F., ed. 1970. "Development of Central Places in the Coast Province, Kenya." Mimeographed. Ottawa: Carleton University.

Taylor, W. E. 1891. *Giriama Vocabulary and Collections*. London: S.P.C.N.

Turner, V. W. 1957. *Schism and Continuity in an African Society*. Manchester University Press.

———. 1968. *The Drums of Affliction*. Oxford: Clarendon.

Watson, W. 1958. *Tribal Cohesion in a Money Economy*. Manchester University Press.

Weber, M. 1930. *The Protestant Ethic and the Spirit of Capitalism*. Trans., Talcott Parsons. New York: Charles Scribner's Sons.

Wilson, F. R. 1949. "Notes on Bridewealth." *Kilifi District Political Record*.

Index